ABC

OF PLAIN WORDS

BY

SIR ERNEST GOWERS

author of Plain Words

LONDON
HIS MAJESTY'S STATIONERY OFFICE
1951

PUBLISHED BY HIS MAJESTY'S STATIONERY OFFICE

To be purchased from

York House, Kingsway, LONDON, W.C.2 429 Oxford Street, LONDON, W.1

P.O. Box 569, LONDON, S.E.1

13a Castle Street, EDINBURGH, 2 1 St. Andrew's Crescent, CARDIFF

39 King Street, MANCHESTER, 2 Tower Lane, BRISTOL, 1

2 Edmund Street, BIRMINGHAM, 3 80 Chichester Street, BELFAST

or from any Bookseller

1951

S.O. Code No. 63-119-1*

Printed in Great Britain under the authority of His Majesty's Stationery Office by Fosh & Cross Ltd., London

PREFACE

Why this Book was Written

THIS book is a supplement to *Plain Words*. Like *Plain Words*, it was written at the invitation of the Treasury to help in improving official English. *Plain Words*, they said, has given us a start; but that is not enough. We must have something that can be kept on the desk and consulted on points of difficulty as they arise. *Plain Words* is of little use for that; it has not even an index. What is now wanted is a reference book with entries under headings alphabetically arranged. There are, it is true, several books of that sort, but they are not in quite the right focus for our purpose. There are plenty of grammar-books too, all with indexes. But these do not quite meet the case either. All contain many things that need not be in the sort of book that we have in mind and omit some things that ought to be there. Would I try my hand at an ABC suitably focused? I said I would, and that is how this book came to be written.

I soon discovered that an ABC lay-out presents two great difficulties to its compiler, and I am not confident of having overcome either. One is that it tends to put everything on the same plane—to give the impression that all the points mentioned are, in the compiler's opinion, of equal importance. Nothing could be further from the truth here. For instance, under the heading NUMBER is some advice about when a singular verb should be used with that word, and when a plural. It is sound advice, and may be useful to those who care about being correct in such things. But I cannot believe it to be of real importance whether anyone writes " a number is " or " a number are ". Whichever he does, his readers will find no difficulty in knowing what he means, and to get it " wrong " is no evidence of any defect in his education or intelligence. On another page will be found a heading ABSTRACT NOUNS. Here examples are given to show how addiction to abstract nouns, that commonest and most pernicious vice of present-day writing, is the result of confused thinking and the cause of woolly circumlocution; and produces a habit of mind (to take the specimen most recently added to my collection) which asks "was this the realisation of an anticipated liability?" when what is meant is "did you expect you would have to do this?" The article on this subject is cardinal, and I should be sorry if anyone thought that I put the one about NUMBER on the same level. That these topics may not appear in proper perspective is the more unfortunate because we do not yet seem to have wholly rid ourselves of the idea, prevalent a generation or two ago, that the unimportant things mattered most, and that a good writer was one who scrupulously observed musty taboos like those that forbid the splitting of the infinitive, the use of *whose* with an inanimate antecedent, or writing *very pleased* or *different to*. All I can do is to disclaim any such purpose; and I hope that perhaps *Plain Words* may continue to be read in conjunction with its sequel, and serve to promote what I think to be the true sense of values.

The other difficulty is more serious. The object of this book is to enable a writer to keep himself straight by looking up the entry that will give him guidance whenever he is in doubt on any point of diction or usage. Over a large part of the field that should be plain sailing. He wants, let us say, to know whether to use *contact* as a verb. He turns to CONTACT, and finds there some advice about it. He is not sure whether a comma is needed in a certain place. He turns to COMMA, knowing that there, if anywhere, he will discover the answer. But what of the writer who needs not a simple and straightforward piece of advice like this, which he knows he wants, but to be saved from falling into some blunder that perhaps he has never heard of? If he knows that what he is about to write is a blunder, he will not write it, and needs no help to avoid it. If he does not know, what will there be to set him questioning? The entry ABSTRACT NOUNS will again serve as an example. There is no reason why anyone addicted to abstract nouns, unconscious of any offence, should ever be prompted to read that article; nor can I think of any other title for it that would be more likely to throw it in his way. An ABC, if used only as a work of reference, will be of no service to such people. And if they are expected to read the book through, why make things harder for them by casting it into the forbidding form of a sort of dictionary?

I have tried to meet this difficulty by prefacing the ABC with a guide to its contents arranged under subjects. This may be of use in steering those who already know what they want guidance about, but its main purpose is to awaken questionings in those who do not, and to show them where any curiosity or misgivings that may have been aroused in them can be put to the test. So I hope that anyone who uses the book will make a point of reading the guide.

As I have said, a new book was thought to be necessary because existing books are not in the right focus for this special purpose. It follows that this book does not profess to be a complete guide to what ought to be known by those who wish to write well. It concentrates on what seem to its compiler to be the weakest points in the use of English today for official and similar purposes, and ignores, or passes lightly over, rules and conventions generally observed. It also avoids as far as possible grammatical jargon, which most of us forget as soon as we leave school; though it is necessary to assume the reader's familiarity with the commonest grammatical terms, such as the names of the parts of speech, the parts of verbs, and the cases. Some of what is in this book is in *Plain Words*; most is not. Almost all the examples are new; like those in *Plain Words* they are drawn in the main from recent official and commercial documents.

The right focus, then, depends on right observation, and as the observation that went to the making of this book was limited to my own and that of one or two others who have been good enough to help me, there can hardly fail to be many shortcomings in it, especially of omission. I shall welcome from readers any criticisms, suggestions, and examples that may improve future editions. I have had many letters about *Plain Words*, all of them kind but most of them criticising something that I had said, and some convicting me of error beyond question. I acknowledge with gratitude the interest and profit that I have derived from these letters. If any curious reader should notice that there are passages in this book that are at variance with what was said in *Plain Words*, he may safely assume the explanation to be that I have been convinced I was wrong.

I have again many helpers to thank. Mr. A. P. Sinker, C.B., lately Director of Training and Education at the Treasury, inspired the book, and kept a guiding hand on its preparation. Miss E. M. Kirk and Miss M. I. P. Norman of his Division have given me invaluable assistance. I have once more been fortunate enough to have the benefit of Mr. Wyn Griffith's wise and frank advice. Mr. L. F. Schooling has spared no trouble to enable me to profit from his experience of training officials in expressing themselves. I had ready co-operation from every government department from whom I asked it, and I owe particular thanks to Miss Oliver of the Board of Trade.

I must also record my gratitude to the authors, publishers, and proprietors of the books, newspapers, and periodicals that I have used and quoted from and especially of the books listed on the opposite page.

THE BOOKS REFERRED TO

(See the Preface p.vi)

FOWLER, H. W. and F. G., *The King's English.*
Oxford University Press. 3rd edn., 1930.

FOWLER, H. W. *A Dictionary of Modern English Usage.*
Oxford University Press, 1926.

HERBERT, A.P. *What a Word!*
Methuen. 1935.

JESPERSEN, O. *Essentials of English Grammar.*
Allen & Unwin, 1933.

The Oxford English Dictionary.
Oxford University Press, 1933.

PARTRIDGE, E. *Usage and Abusage.*
Hamish Hamilton. 4th edn., 1948.

PARTRIDGE, E. *A Dictionary of Clichés.*
Routledge & Kegan Paul. 4th edn., 1950.

PERRIN, P. G., *Writer's Guide and Index to English.*
New York. Scott. 1942.

TREBLE, H. A. and VALLINS, G. H. *An A.B.C. of English Usage.*
Oxford University Press, 1936.

WESEEN, Maurice H., *Words Confused and Misused.*
Pitman. 1948.

WHITTEN, W., and WHITAKER, F. *Good and Bad English.*
Newnes. 2nd edn., 1950.

How to Use the ABC

THIS book is made up of articles on subjects about which inexperienced writers may need guidance. As the title of the book shows, the articles are arranged in the alphabetical order of their subjects. Many are about the proper use of certain words or phrases. Among these you should have no difficulty in finding what you want. If you are in doubt about the correct use of *alibi* or *anticipate*, all you have to do is to turn up those entries ; if you feel that you are overworking *overall* or *alternative*, you will find under those headings other words that might suit you better.

But some articles are concerned with more general topics. The " subject " that determines the place of one of these in the book may be some point of grammar or style. For instance, under ABSTRACT WORDS is a warning against using them too much, under ING ENDINGS something is said about the pitfalls by which participles and gerunds are beset, and under GOBBLEDYGOOK—a pleasant and expressive new word of American invention—there is a description of a way of writing that you would do well to avoid. You are not likely to turn up any of these headings of your own accord, except perhaps by accident. How are you to know under which heading to look for guidance when you are not sure how to define your problem to yourself—perhaps do not even know that you have a problem ? There can be no complete answer to this question, but the following analysis has been made in the hope that it may help readers to find their way about.

The articles in the book can be classified roughly under four main labels—VOCABULARY, GRAMMAR, MECHANICS, and STYLE, concerning themselves with the four questions:

I. Am I using a word or phrase in its proper sense ?
II. Is my grammar right ?
III. Is what I have written properly constructed and punctuated and spelt ?
IV. Is what I have written as clear and as simple as it can be made ?

In the lists comprised in this analysis, the contents of the A.B.C. are grouped under these four headings, and the articles that fall into the first three groups are further sub-divided by subject. If you read these lists, or any set of them that you think most likely to give you what you want, they will suggest to you headings under which to look in the A.B.C. for guidance. Perhaps they may even reveal to you an unsuspected need for guidance.

I. VOCABULARY:

This group can be divided into three:

(i) *Words and phrases liable to be used superfluously, unsuitably, or wrongly*

Here is a list of words of this sort that you will find in the A.B.C.:

Achieve
Adumbrate
Advert
Advise
Aggravate
Alibi
Alternative
And/or
Angle (see Point of View)
Anticipate
Appreciate
Apprise
Approximately
A priori
Apt (see Likely)
As and As From
As and when
As to
Aspect
Assist
Availability
Background
Backlog
Basis
Beg (to inform)
Beg the question
Bilateral (see Unilateral, etc.)
Bottleneck
Brackets
Breakdown
Calculated (see Likely)
Case
Ceiling
Character
Claim
Collusion
Commence
Comparatively (see Relatively, etc.)
Concerned (so far as . . . is)
Confirm
Connexion (in this connexion)
Considerable
Consideration (under consideration)
Contact (as a verb)
Course (of course)
Deadline
Dearth (see Lack)
Decimate
Deem
Definite(ly)
Desiderate and Desideratum
Desire
Develop
Dilemma
Distant (not too distant)
Donate
End (to this end)
Entail
Envisage
Essential
Evacuate
Event and Eventuality
Eventuate
Evince
Experience (as a verb)
Fact (the fact that)
Far [so far as . . . concerned] (see concerned)
Favour (for favour of)
Feasible
Feature
Following (as a preposition)
Former and Latter
Fraction (see Percentage, etc.)
Function (as a verb)
Furthermore
Global
Got
Group
Hand (to hand)
Help (more than one can help)
Hereto and Herewith, etc.
Idem (see Inst., etc.)
If (for though or whether)
If and when
Implement
Inasmuch as
Incidentally
Inclined to think
Inculcate
Individual
Inform
Infers (see Imply)

Information (for your information)
Instance
Inst., Ult., Prox., Idem.
Involve
Item
Lack and Dearth
Latter (see Former)
Leading question
Liable (see Likely)
Likely
Limited
Liquidate and Liquidation
Literally
Loan
Locate and Location
Major
Majority
Materialise
Means
Meticulous
Multilateral (see Unilateral, etc.)
Mutual
Occasion (as a verb)
Optimistic
Otherwise
Overall (as an adjective)
Particular
Per
Percentage, Proportion, Fraction
Peruse
Phenomenal
Please find
Point of view, etc.
Position (as a noun)
Position (as a verb)
Position (not in a)
Prepared to
Prior to
Prone (see Likely)
Proportion (see Percentage, etc.)
Proposition
Protagonist
Provided that
Prox. (see Inst., etc.)
Purport (as a noun)
Purport (as a verb)
Question
Re
Reaction
Realistic
Recrudescence
Redundant
Relatively and Comparatively (and Unduly)
Rendition
Require
Respective(ly)
Sabotage
Same
Service (as a verb)
Short supply
Special pleading
Specific
Standpoint (see Point of view)
Steps (take)
Sterilise
Substitute
Such
Such Time As [Until and During] (see Until)
Sufficient
Target
Thereto, Therewith, etc. (see Hereto, Herewith, etc.)
Transmit
Transpire
Ult. (see Inst., etc.)
Unduly (see Relatively, etc.)
Unilateral, Multilateral, Bilateral
Until (Unless and until, until such time)
Utilise and Utilisation
Very
Viewpoint (see Point of View)
While
Worth (while)

(ii) *Pairs of words liable to be confused*

Each of the following pairs will be found in the A.B.C. under the first word of the pair.

Adherence *and* Adhesion
Affect *and* Effect
Alternate *and* Alternative
Autarchy *and* Autarky

Averse *and* Adverse
Compare to *and* Compare with
Comprise *and* Compose
Consequent *and* Consequential
Consist in *and* Consist of
Continual *and* Continuous
Defective *and* Deficient
Definitive *and* Definite
Dependant *and* Dependent
Deprecate *and* Depreciate
Direct *and* Directly
Disassociate *and* Dissociate
Disinterested *and* Uninterested
Disposal *and* Disposition
Draftsman *and* Draughtsman
e.g. *and* i.e.
Enquiry *and* Inquiry
Factitious *and* Fictitious
Forego *and* Forgo
Hard *and* Hardly
Imply *and* Infer
Less *and* Fewer
Meantime *and* Meanwhile
Practical *and* Practicable
Resort, Resource *and* Recourse
Verbal *and* Oral
Waste *and* Wastage

(iii) *Certain present-day trends in the behaviour of words*

The English vocabulary is constantly changing: words acquire new meanings; new words are invented; old ones disappear. The following four articles deal with current tendencies of this sort:

Changes in the meaning of words
De and Dis (use of as prefixes, e.g., decontaminate)
New Verbs
Non (use of as prefix)

II. GRAMMAR:

To help you in finding guidance on points of grammar, here is an index in nine classified groups:

(i) Verbs, Their Moods and Tenses

Ing endings (points relating to gerunds and participles, absolute construction, the unrelated participle, the fused participle, and other matters,
Shall and Will
Subjunctive (uses of)
Tenses, Sequence of tenses (I should be glad if you would)
Verbs, omission of
Would

(ii) Pronouns

Each
Either
One
Pronouns (use of)
Repetition
Same (as a pronoun)
Such
That
They for He or She
(*See also* RELATIVES *below*)

(iii) Relatives

Comma (for the difference between commenting and defining relative clauses)
That
What
When
Which
Which and That
Who and Whom
Whose

(iv) The Cases

I and Me (It's me : Between you and I)
Than (than whom)
What (in two cases at once)
Which (in two cases at once)
Who and Whom

(v) Number (Singular or Plural)

Agenda
Collective words
Data
Each
Either
Follows (as follows)
Kind (these kind of)
Majority
Many a
Means
More than one
Neither . . . nor
None
Number
Singular and Plural Verbs (general article on subjects taking singular or plural verbs)
Sort (*see* Kind)
There is (and There are)
They for He or She
What

(vi) Negatives

Negative (double negatives)

Neither . . . nor
Non (as a prefix)
None
Nor and or
Un- (confusion caused by)

(vii) Duplication

Double passives
Negative (double negative)
One
Overlapping (The reason is because, etc.)
That (carelessly repeated)

(viii) Miscellaneous Rules and Conventions

And (beginning a sentence)
And which (proper use of)
Circumstances (in or under)
First (or firstly)
First two (or two first)
Idiom
Preposition (at end of sentence)
Split infinitive
Very (very pleased)
Whose (used of things)

(ix) Words That Set Grammatical Traps

Aim
As
As to
Avail
Averse
Because
Between
Both
But
Capable
Compare
Consist
Depend
Differ
Different
Doubt
Due to
Entail
Equally
Even
Following
Follows (as follows)
Forecast
Hope
If
Inform
Kind
Like
Not (not all ; not . . . but)
One
Only
Order (in order that)
Otherwise
Prefer
Prepositions (cannibalism by)
Prevent
Prohibit
Purport (as a verb)
Regard
Sort (see Kind)
Such (such as, such that, such and so)
That
The more, etc.
Unequal
Very
Worth (worth while)
Write

III. MECHANICS:

(i) For help in matters of *construction* see the headings:

Letters (framework and construction)
Paragraphing
Sentences

(ii) For help in *punctuation* see the headings :

Apostrophe
Colon

Comma
Dash
Full Stop
Hyphen
Inverted commas
Semicolon

(iii) And on a point of *spelling* see

Ise or ize

IV. STYLE:

Articles that give guidance about this and are not easily classifiable under any more specific label are :—

Abstract words (addiction to)
Adjectives (proper use of)
Adverbs (proper use of)
Arrangement
Cliché
Commercialese
Explanation (what to aim at and what to avoid in explaining)
Gobbledygook (a general section)
Idiom
Jargon
Metaphor
Noun adjectives
Padding
Parenthesis
Phrasal verbs
Prepositions (circumlocutory substitutes for)
Qualification of Absolutes (very unique)
Sentences
Verbal particles (*see* Phrasal verbs)

ABC OF PLAIN WORDS

ABSTRACT WORDS

An abstract noun denotes something intangible—a quality or state; a concrete noun denotes the person or thing that may possess that quality or be in that state. Thus *man* is concrete and *humanity* abstract, *brain* concrete and *thought* abstract. Abstract nouns are indispensable in their proper places. But one of the greatest faults of present-day writing is to use them to excess. There are two reasons why this is bad. First, it means that statements are made in a roundabout instead of a direct way, and the meaning is more difficult to grasp. The commonest form of roundabout is to make an abstract noun the subject of a sentence which would be clearer and more natural if its subject were a concrete noun or a personal pronoun—to say, for example, " was this the realisation of an anticipated liability ? " instead of " did you expect you would have to do this ? " Secondly, abstract nouns have less precise meanings than concrete ones, and therefore should be avoided as far as possible by those who wish to make their meaning plain. There is not room for wide variation in the interpretation by different people of such words as *house* and *ship*. But there is infinite room for differences of opinion about what is meant by such words as *liberty* and *democracy*.

Unfortunately the very vagueness of abstract words is one of the reasons for their popularity. To express one's thoughts accurately is hard work, and to be precise is sometimes dangerous. We are tempted to prefer the safer obscurity of the abstract. To resist this temptation, and to resolve to make your meaning plain to your reader even at the cost of some trouble to yourself, is more important than any other single thing if you would convert a flabby style into a crisp one. As Mr. G. M. Young has said, an excessive reliance on the noun at the expense of the verb will, in the end, detach the mind of the writer from the realities of here and now, from when and how and in what mood the thing was done, and insensibly induce a habit of abstraction, generalisation and vagueness.

Here are five examples of the roundabout abstract phrase and two of sentences which have been made almost unintelligible by an excessive reliance on abstract words.

ROUNDABOUT PHRASES

Your entitlement to full benefit is apparent. (You are clearly entitled to full benefit.)

The cessation of the present restrictions cannot be made. (The present restrictions cannot be lifted.)

Early expectancy of a vacancy is given by the firm. (The firm expect to have a vacancy soon.)

Complete restoration of the surface results within a few weeks. (The surface is completely restored within a few weeks.)

A wide age differentiation is apparent among the entrants. (The entrants are of widely different ages.)

The extent of diversion of ships to other ports is not known. (It is not known how many ships have been diverted to other ports.)

EXCESSIVE USE OF ABSTRACT NOUNS

The desirability of attaining unanimity so far as the general construction of the body is concerned is of considerable importance from the production aspect.

The actualisation of the motivation of the forces must to a great extent be a matter of personal angularity.

The meaning of these two can only be conjectured.

Sometimes abstract words are actually invented, so powerful is the lure of saying things this way.

The reckonability of former temporary service for higher leave entitlement.

See also Position. *Position* and *situation* are notable snares. Indeed all words ending in *tion* should be treated as suspects and passed only after being questioned.

ACHIEVE

This word implies successful effort, and should not be treated as merely the equivalent of *getting* or *reaching*, as in the phrase, which I believe is not unknown, "Officers achieving redundancy". There is an air of dignity about *achieve* which may lead writers astray and produce sentences like "this was impossible of achievement", in preference to the simpler "this could not be done".

ADHERENCE AND ADHESION

Either of these words can be used in the figurative sense of adhering (say) to a political party, but only *adhesion* in the literal sense of one substance sticking to another.

ADJECTIVES

It has been wisely said that the adjective is the enemy of the noun. If we seldom see the noun *danger* except in company with *real* or *serious* we think less of it than it deserves when we find it standing by itself. If we make a habit of saying " The true facts are these ", we shall come under suspicion when we profess to tell merely " the facts ". If a *crisis* is always *acute* and an *emergency* always *grave*, what is left for those words to do by themselves? If *active* constantly accompanies *consideration*, we shall think we are being fobbed off when we are promised bare consideration. If a decision is always qualified by *definite*, a decision by itself becomes a poor filleted thing. If conditions are customarily described as *prerequisite* or *essential*, we shall doubt whether a *condition* without an adjective is really a condition at all.

Cultivate the habit of reserving adjectives to make your meaning more precise, and suspect those that you find yourself using to make it more emphatic. Be on your guard against slipping into that automatic sort of writing in which every test is acid and every moment psychological. Use adjectives to denote kind rather than degree. By all means say an *economic crisis* or a *military disaster*, but think well before saying an *acute crisis* or a *terrible disaster*. Say if you like " The proposal met with noisy opposition and is in obvious danger of defeat ". But do not say " The proposal met with considerable opposition and is in real danger of defeat ". If that is all you want to say it is better to leave out the adjectives and say " The proposal met with opposition and is in danger of defeat ".

Beware in particular of pushful adjectives of vague intensification, such as *considerable*, *appreciable* and *substantial*. None of these three should ever be used without three questions being first asked. Do I need an adjective at all? If so, would not a more specific adjective suit better? If not, which of these three words (with their different shades of meaning) serves my purpose best? Have we not reached the stage when " This is urgent " sounds more urgent than " This is a matter of considerable urgency "?

ADUMBRATE

This word is too much used. *Sketch*, *outline* or *foreshadow* may do for a change.

ADVERBS

Adverbs answer in advance the question " how ", or " when ", or " where ", or " to what extent ", or " why ", by giving such replies as " precisely ", " today ", " here ", " completely ", and " consequently ". There are also " adverbs of assertion " (e.g. " yes ", " no ", " perhaps ") and " introductory adverbs " (e.g. " accordingly ", " however ").*

---

* Perrin, *Writer's Guide*, sb. ADVERB.

But your reader is often uninterested in the answers to these questions, especially when you answer in an uncertain voice with some invertebrate adverb like *unduly* or *substantially.* The bare statement is all he wants. What has been said under the heading ADJECTIVES is equally true of adverbs. Be sparing of them, and use them to give precision rather than to add emphasis. Distrust all those that vaguely intensify, such as *very*, *considerably*, *appreciably*, *unduly* and *substantially*, and those that vaguely mitigate such as *relatively*, *comparatively*, *duly*, *somewhat*, *rather*. The unreflecting use of *very* is a bad habit easily acquired.

So is the insertion of *necessarily* or *inevitably* into a plain statement of fact. *Inevitably* is much in vogue just now. It adds nothing in these examples :

> The Committees will inevitably have a part to play in the development of the service.
>
> The ultimate power of control which flows inevitably from the agency relationship.

See RELATIVELY, RESPECTIVELY, SOMEWHAT, UNDULY, VERY.

On the position of adverbs, *see* EVEN, ONLY, SPLIT INFINITIVE.

ADVERSE *see* AVERSE

ADVERT

> Adverting to my letter of the 7th August, 1947, I have to inform you that. . . .

Do not begin a letter like that. *Advert* (except as a slang contraction of *advertisement*) is now an archaic word, and to start a letter with it is to create an atmosphere of primness which you will not easily dispel.

ADVISE

The use of *advise* in the sense of *inform* or *tell* brings a flavour of commercialese (*see* that heading) and stiffness into a letter. None could object to *advise* in:

> If you are in doubt on any point I shall be glad to advise you,

but

> I have not received any advice that your promise has been implemented

would have been better expressed " I have not heard that you have kept your promise ".

AFFECT and EFFECT

Effect is both a noun and a verb. As a verb it means to *bring about*, to *accomplish*. As a noun it means primarily something caused or produced, a *result*, a *consequence*. *Affect* is only a verb:

its use as a noun is obsolete or technical. The most common meaning of *affect* is *have an effect on.* Thus we may say either " that does not affect my plans " or " that has no effect on my plans ", and mean the same thing. But " my plans are affected " means almost the opposite of " my plans are effected ". The second indicates accomplishment of the plans, the first an obstacle to their accomplishment.

Because *affect* is a colourless word it has won an undeserved popularity. It is of the class of *factor*, *issue*, *involve* (*see* INVOLVE)—a word of broad meaning that saves a writer the trouble of close thought. It is a useful word in its place, but it should not be used from laziness. Do not say " the progress of the building has been *affected* by the weather ", but prefer a more precise word, *hindered*, perhaps, or *delayed* or *stopped*.

AGENDA

Agenda, though in form plural, has been admitted to the language as a singular word. Nobody would say " the agenda for Monday's meeting *have* not yet reached me ". If a word is needed for one of the components of the agenda, say " item No. so-and-so of the agenda " not " agendum No. so-and-so ", which would be the extreme of pedantry.

AGGRAVATE

The use of this word in the sense of *annoy*, though there is good authority for it, has not won general acceptance and offends some readers. In official writing, therefore, the word should be used only in its etymological sense of *make worse*.

AIM

> The Ministry of Transport aim to reduce substantially the number of uncontrolled crossings.
>
> The Ministry of Health has asked local authorities to aim for immunisation of three out of every four babies before reaching their first year.

The idiomatic construction with *aim* is *aim at doing*, and not (as here) *aim to do* or *aim for* something.

ALIBI

> There is still a minority of our membership which has failed to recognise its new responsibilities. It is not sufficient to point to

certain shortcomings of the National Coal Board to create an alibi.

Members of the timber trade, like members of any other trade, are glad of any alibi to explain any particular increases in price.

Either we accept the bare facts or we go down to a lower standard of living. The day of alibis is gone.

Do not use *alibi* as it is used in these examples, in the sense of *excuse*, or of an admission of guilt with a plea of extenuating circumstances, or of throwing the blame on someone else. *Alibi* is the Latin for *elsewhere*. To plead an alibi is to rebut a charge by adducing evidence that the person charged was elsewhere at the time of the act alleged against him. " Oh Sammy Sammy vy vornt there an alleybi ? " cried old Mr. Weller at the conclusion of *Bardell* v. *Pickwick* (in which it was beyond dispute that Mrs. Bardell had been found in Mr. Pickwick's embrace) and so furnished a classic example of the confusing properties of this word.

ALTERNATE and ALTERNATIVE

These two words are often confused. *Alternate(ly)* means by turns. *Alternative(ly)* means in a way that offers a choice. " The journey may be made by rail or alternately by road " means, if it means anything, that every other journey may be made by road. It does not mean, as the writer intended, that for every journey the traveller has a choice between the two means of transport. Conversely " alternatively they sat and walked in the moonlight, talking of this and that " cannot have been intended to mean that they sat and walked in the moonlight as an alternative to doing something else ; what must have been intended is that they sat and walked alternately. *Alternate* can also be a verb meaning, in popular language, to " take it in turns ".

See also next heading.

ALTERNATIVE

This word should only be used when a choice may be made. It has recently been driving out other more suitable words, and constantly appears where there is no choice, and the proper word is some such adjective as *other*, *fresh*, *different*, *revised*, *substitute*. Possibly this strange popularity comes from the attractive jingle " alternative accommodation ", sanctioned by the legislature, in the sense of accommodation other than that already occupied. Mistrust *alternative* deeply : always ask yourself whether there is in fact a choice, and if there is not, select some other word.

The Parliamentary Secretary said that it was perfectly proper for the Minister to comment on the findings of an inquiry, and to take an alternative view. (Different.)

I thank you for your letter and note that you have made alternative arrangements respecting the pulleys. (Other.)

It is noted that you are seeking alternative employment. (That you are looking for other work.)

The Minister regrets that he will not be able to hold the Conference arranged for the 15th March. Members will be informed as soon as alternative arrangements have been made. (Fresh.)

To provide alternative storage in place of that destroyed by enemy action. (*Alternative* is here meaningless and should be omitted.)

It is pedantry to say that, because of its derivation, *alternative* must not be used where the choices are more than two. *See* CHANGES IN THE MEANING OF WORDS.

AND

There used to be an idea that it was inelegant to begin a sentence with *and*. The idea is now as good as dead. And to use *and* in this position may be a useful way of indicating that what you are about to say will reinforce what you have just said.

AND/OR

This ugly and unnecessary symbol is only fit for forms and lists and specifications and things of that sort ; it should find no place in any document that has any pretence to literary form. It can always be dispensed with. Instead of writing (say) " soldiers and/or sailors " we can write " soldiers or sailors or both ". Moreover, whatever claim may be made on behalf of *and/or* as a saver of space and time, there can be no possible justification for using it where *or* by itself is enough, as it is in :

Professional fees should be included when paid to any architect, surveyor or engineer acting as such in an advisory and/or supervisory capacity.

AND WHICH

There is a grammarians' rule that it is wrong to write *and which* (and similar expressions such as *and who*, *and where*, *but which*, *or which*, etc.) except by way of introducing a second relative clause with the same antecedent as one that has just preceded it. According to this rule, Nelson was wrong grammatically, as well as in other more momentous ways, when he wrote to Lady Nelson after his first introduction to Lady Hamilton:

> She is a young woman of amiable manners and who does honour to the station to which he has raised her.

To justify the *and who* grammatically a relative is needed in the first part of the sentence, for example,

> She is a young woman whose manners are amiable and who etc.

Conversely, the writer of the following sentence has got into trouble by being shy of *and which:*

> Things which we ourselves could not produce and yet are essential to our recovery.

Here *which* cannot double the parts of object of *produce* and subject of *are*. To set the grammar right the relative has to be repeated:

> Things which we ourselves could not produce and which are etc.

The rule is subject to many exceptions and complications. Fowler has nine columns on it. Those who observe it in the simple form in which it is stated at the beginning of this section may at least be sure of not offending the purists. But they will do still better if they resolve to avoid the inevitable clumsiness of *and which*, even when grammatical. Thus these two sentences might be written:

> She is a young woman of amiable manners who does honour to the station to which he has called her.
>
> Things essential to our recovery which we ourselves could not produce.

ANGLE *see* POINT OF VIEW

ANTICIPATE

Do not write *anticipate* when you mean *expect*. Confine *anticipate* to its proper meaning of forestalling something. "I anticipated your request" does not mean merely that I expected it; it means that I have complied with it in advance.

Anticipate is wrongly used in:

> There are no vacancies at present; nor are any anticipated for some time,

and

> It is anticipated to complete the work in about ten days.

It is rightly used in:

> The Chancellor of the Exchequer said that he could not anticipate his budget statement,

and:

> Remember, in conducting, that your thought and gesture will almost certainly be too late rather than too early. Anticipate everything.

"Thanking you in anticipation" uses the word correctly but falls under the ban of commercialese. *See* COMMERCIALESE.

The use of *anticipate* for *expect* is now so general that it may soon have to be recognised as idiomatic. But it would be a pity not to fight to the last against so wanton a corruption of a word possessing a precise and useful meaning of its own.

APOSTROPHE

The only functions of the apostrophe that call for notice are (*a*) its use to denote the possessive of names ending in *s* and of pronouns, (*b*) its use before a final *s* to show that the *s* is forming the plural of a word or symbol not ordinarily admitting of a plural, and (*c*) its use in defining periods of time.

(*a*) There is no universally accepted code of rules governing the formation of the possessive case of words ending in s, but the most favoured practice seems to be not just to put an apostrophe at the end of the word, as one does with an ordinary plural (strangers' gallery), but to add another s—Mr. Jones's room, St. James's street, not Mr. Jones' room, St. James' street.

As to pronouns, all these except the pronoun *one* dispense with an apostrophe in their possessive cases—*hers*, *yours*, *theirs*, *ours* and *its*, but *one's*, not *ones*. *It's* is not the possessive of *it* but a contraction of *it is*.

(*b*) Whether an apostrophe should be used to denote the plural of a word or symbol that does not ordinarily make a plural depends on whether the plural is readily recognisable as such. Unless the reader really needs help it should not be thrust upon him. It is clearly justified with single letters: "there are two o's in woolly"; "mind your p's and q's". Otherwise it is rarely called for. It should not be used with contractions (e.g. M.P.s) or merely because what is put into the plural is not a noun. Editors of Shakespeare do without it in "Tellest thou me of ifs". and Rudyard Kipling did not think it necessary in:

> One million Hows, two million Wheres,
> And seven million Whys.

(*c*) Whether one should use an apostrophe or not in such expressions as "Ten years imprisonment" is a disputed and not very important point. Each can be justified : *Ten years'* on the ground that the phrase means "imprisonment of ten years", and so *years* must be in the possessive case ; *ten years* on the ground that it is an adjectival phrase. The ordinary practice seems to be to use the apostrophe for the singular ("a week's interval") but not for the plural ("a six weeks interval").

APPRECIATE

The ordinary meaning of *appreciate*, as a transitive verb, is to form an estimate of the worth of anything, to set a value on it. It is therefore not surprising that it is useful to polite officials corresponding with members of the public who want more than they can get, as most of us do to-day. Refusals are softened by such phrases as "I appreciate how hard it is on you not to have it", and "you will appreciate the reasons why I cannot let you have it". Whatever the reason, there can be no doubt that *appreciate* is being used by the writers of official letters and circulars with a freedom that passes reason and needs to be curbed. An effective way of curbing it might be to resolve never to use it with a *that* clause ("I appreciate that there has been delay"), but always give it a noun or noun-clause ("I appreciate your kindness").

Sometimes the word is used merely by way of polite padding (*see* PADDING) as in:

> You will appreciate therefore that the earliest date the department can release you is . . .
>
> It will no doubt be appreciated that this cannot be reserved for an indefinite period.

The first might just as well have begun "The earliest date therefore" and the second "this cannot of course be reserved . . ." or, if that seems too abrupt, "You will no doubt understand that . . ."

Appreciate is often used where it would be more suitable to say *understand*, *realise*, *recognise*, *be grateful*, *be obliged*.

"It would be appreciated if" can usually be translated into "I shall be glad (or grateful, or obliged, or even pleased) if . . .". "You will appreciate" can often be better expressed by "you will realise", or even "of course". Here are extracts from two letters that say the same thing, one with the help of *appreciate* and the other without. The one that does without is more natural and vigorous:

> I fully appreciate that, in the circumstances you mention, a telephone would be a great convenience to you.
>
> I realise just how useful a telephone would be to you.

APPRISE

Apprise is an old-fashioned word and gives a stilted air to a letter when it is used as a synonym for *tell*, *inform*, or *notify*. The use of *apprise* in the sense of *appraise* (put a value on) is now confined to Scottish law, and should be kept there.

APPROXIMATELY

Do not let this grand word make you forget the existence of humbler words like *roughly* and *about*:

> It is understood that Mr. X spent some time in America, approximately from 1939 to 1946.

Roughly would be both more homely and more appropriate in its meaning.

A PRIORI

Do not say *a priori* when you mean *prima facie* ; in fact you can probably get on without either.

> Several countries most advanced from a medical point of view have for the last 20 years done without this drug, " a fact ", says the Board, " which is sufficient to show that there is an a priori case for its total abolition ".

No—it does not. To argue *a priori* is to argue from assumed axioms and not from experience. The argument here rests on the 20-year experience of several countries, and so is an argument *a posteriori*.

Prima facie, which is what the writer probably had in mind, means on a first impression, before hearing fully the evidence for and against.

APT *see* LIKELY

ARRANGEMENT

Putting words in their proper places is all-important in a language which, except in some of its pronouns, does not have different forms for the subjective and objective cases. With those pronouns arrangement is not so vital. Neither " he outlived her " nor " her he outlived " leaves any doubt which outlived the other. But with nouns the meaning depends rigidly on the order. " Husband outlived wife " means one thing and " wife outlived husband " the opposite. Reverse the order of the words and you reverse the meaning.

If all you want to say is a simple thing like that, there is no difficulty. But that is rarely so. You probably want to write a more complicated sentence telling not only the central event but also its how, why, and where. The Americans have a useful word, *modifier*, by which they mean " words or groups of words that restrict, limit, or make more exact the meaning of other words ". The ' modifiers ' bring the trouble.

The rule is easy enough to state. It is, in the words of an old grammarian, " that the words or members most nearly related should be placed in the sentence as near to each other as possible, so as to make their mutual relation clearly appear ". But it is not so easy to keep. We do not always remember that what is clear to us may be far from clear to our readers. Sometimes it is not clear even to us which " words or members " are " most nearly related ", and if there are many 'modifiers' we may be confronted with difficulties of the jig-saw type.

Here are some typical examples of faulty arrangement. Their offence is that they obscure the writer's meaning, if only momentarily :

> It is doubtful whether this small gas company would wish to accept responsibility for supplying this large area with all its difficulties.

" With all its difficulties " should be put in parenthetic commas after " responsibility ".

> Sir W. S. has cut short the tour that he has been making for the last month in the middle east because of illness.

" Because of illness " should begin the sentence instead of ending it.

Faulty arrangement of this sort is not unknown even in model regulations issued by government departments to show local authorities how things ought to be done :

> No child shall be employed on any weekday when the school is not open for a longer period than four hours.

" For a longer period than four hours " qualifies *employed*, not *open*, and should come immediately after *employed*.

And in departmental regulations themselves:

Every woman by whom . . . a claim for maternity benefit is made shall furnish evidence that she has been, or that it is to be expected that she will be, confined by means of a certificate given in accordance with the rules. . . .

The next example is of a slightly different sort of error:

The operation is carried out in an endeavour to return to its rightful place, 20 acres of soil underlying 18 ins. of dredging from an adjacent dyke.

Here the writer, puzzled where to put " to its rightful place " without creating an ambiguity, has welded it into an impossibly clumsy verb with *return* (" return-to-its-rightful-place ") and has tried to help things out with an impossible comma. The sentence needs recasting, e.g. " The operation is carried out in an endeavour to return 20 acres of soil to its rightful place ; it is now under 18 inches, etc.".

On the practice of trying to remedy faulty arrangement by commas, *see* Comma.

In the next example the writer has lumbered ponderously along without looking where he was going and arrived at the object (*officers*) of the verb *are employing* with a disconcerting bump:

One or two of the largest Local Authorities are at present employing on their staff as certifying officers and as advisers to the Mental Deficiency Act Committees officers having special qualification or experience in mental deficiency.

He would have given himself little more trouble, and would have saved his reader some, if he had turned the sentence round and written:

Officers having special qualification or experience in mental deficiency are at present being employed on the staff of one or two of the largest Local Authorities as certifying officers and as advisers to the Mental Deficiency Act Committees.

Other common errors of arrangement which are likely to give the reader unnecessary trouble, if they do not actually bewilder him, are letting the relative get a long way from its antecedent and the auxiliary a long way from the main verb. Examples:

(Of relative separated from antecedent.)

Arrangements have been made for the clerk of the Executive Committee to forward a supply of special forms, to whom applications for supplies of such forms should normally be made.

This would have been clearer if the writer had said:

> The clerk to the Executive Committee has been asked to send you a supply of special forms, and you should ask him for more when you want them.

(Of verb separated from auxiliary.)

> The Executive Council should, in the case of approved institutions employing one doctor, get into touch with the committee.
>
> The Council should accordingly, after considering whether they wish to suggest any modifications in the model scheme, consult with the committee. . . .

It is a bad habit to put all sorts of things between the auxiliary and the verb in this way ; it leads to unwieldy sentences and irritated readers.

AS and AS FROM

As has the reputation of being overworked by officials. Dr. Ballard writes:

> The word *as* has acquired a wide vogue in official circles. Wherever *as* can be put in, in it goes. A man in the public service used to draw his salary from a certain date ; now he draws it as from a certain date. Time was when officials would refer to " the relationship between one department and another " ; now they call it " the relationship as between one department and another ". Agenda papers too often include as an item : " to consider as to the question of ". If this sort of interpolation between the verb and its object were extended to ordinary speech, a man would no longer " eat his dinner " but " eat as to his dinner " ; or, to make the parallel complete, " eat as to the diet of his dinner ".

There is reason in saying, of a past date, " these allowances will be payable as from the 1st January last ", but there is none in saying, of a future date, " these allowances will cease to be payable as from the 1st July next ". " On the 1st July " is all that is needed. The phrase " as and from ", not unknown, is mere gibberish.

There are one or two other ways in which *as* may give trouble:

(i) It must not be used as a preposition, on the analogy of *but*. *See* BUT. You may say " no one knows the full truth but me ", but you must not say " no one knows the truth as fully as me ". It must be " as fully as I ". The first *as* is an adverb and the second a conjunction.

(ii) We say " as good *as* ever " and " better *than* ever ". But should we use *as* or *than*, or both, if we say " as good or better " ? The natural thing to say is " as good or better than ever " ignoring the *as* that *as good* logically needs, and you commit no great crime if that is what you do. But if you want both to run no risk of offending the purists and to avoid the prosy " as good as or better than ", you can write " as good as ever or better ". Thus you could change:

> Pamphlets have circulated as widely, and been not less influential, than those published in this volume,

into

> Pamphlets have circulated as widely as those published in this volume, and have been not less influential.

(iii) Do not use the exotic *qua* in places where a simple *as* would do as well. You will be suspected with reason of showing off. *As* is all that is needed in:

> It is requested that the Local Authority will say whether the Local Authority holds the fund qua trustee or otherwise.

AS and WHEN

Like *if and when* (*see* that heading) this pair is rarely if ever justified ; one by itself would meet the case. It might be argued that *as and when* is an appropriate expression to use of something that will happen piecemeal (" Interim reports will be published as and when they are received ") but the argument is not convincing : *as* by itself would do. Nothing can be said for the use of the pair in such a sentence as:

> As and when the Bill becomes an Act guidance will be given on the financial provisions of it as they affect hospital maintenance.

Bills cannot become Acts piecemeal.

AS TO

As to lays two traps for the lazy or careless writer.

(i) Like many other prepositional phrases (e.g. *as regards*, *in connexion with*, *in relation to*, *in the case of*) (*see* PREPOSITIONS) it offers itself as a trouble-saver to those who cannot be bothered to think of the right preposition to express their meaning. For instance:

> Until then it will not be possible to give any indication as to the outcome (of).
>
> A decision has yet to be taken as to this (on or about).

Or it may tempt the writer into a more elaborate circumlocution:

> The operation is a severe one as to the after-effects. (The after-effects of the operation are severe.)
>
> It is no concern of the Ministry as to the source of the information. (The source of the information is no concern of the Ministry.)

(ii) *As to* has a way of intruding itself where it is not wanted, especially before such words as *whether*, *who*, *what*, *how*. All the following examples are better without *as to*:

> Doubt has been expressed as to whether these rewards are sufficient.
>
> I have received an enquiry as to whether you have applied for a supplement to your pension.
>
> I am to ask for some explanation as to why so small a sum was realised on sale.
>
> I will look into the question as to whether you are liable.

As to has several legitimate uses, but they are tricky. A sound rule is never to use it except at the beginning of a sentence by way of introducing a fresh subject:

> As to your liability for previous years, I will go into this and write further to you.

ASPECT

Aspect is the complement of *point of view*. As one changes one's point of view one sees a different aspect of what one is looking at. It is therefore natural that *aspect* should lead writers into the same traps as do *point of view*, *viewpoint* and *standpoint*. *See* POINT OF VIEW. It induces writers, through its vagueness, to prefer it to more precise words, and it lends itself to woolly circumlocution. I cannot believe that there was any clear conception in the head of the official who wrote " They must accept responsibility for the more fundamental aspects of the case ". There is not the same obscurity about " the independence of the Teaching Hospitals is also of considerable importance from the aspect of finance ", but the thought would have been more clearly expressed: " the independence of the Teaching Hospitals is also important financially ".

Aspect is one of the words that should not be used without deliberation, and it should always be rejected if its only function is, as in the last example, to make a clumsy paraphrase of an adverb.

ASSIST

Do not use the word *assist* unless you have some better reason for doing so than that it seems more dignified than *help*.

AUTARCHY and AUTARKY

Autarchy means absolute sovereignty. *Autarky* (sometimes misspelt *autarchy*) means self-sufficiency. The difference in spelling reflects the different Greek words from which they are derived.

AVAIL

The proper construction is to avail oneself of something. Avoid the ugly passive construction such as " this opportunity should be availed of ". " Taken " or " seized " or " made use of " will do instead.

AVAILABILITY

This abstract word contributes much to the prevalent habit of preferring abstract roundabouts to direct speech. *See* ABSTRACT WORDS.

> We would point out that availabilities of this particular material are extremely limited. (. . . that this material is extremely scarce.)

> (On the unnecessary *particular*, *see* PARTICULAR.)

> A despatch has been sent requesting information on the availability of the facilities required . . . (asking how far the required facilities are available.)

> The actual date of the completion of the purchase should coincide with the availability of the new facilities. (The purchase should not be completed until the new facilities are available.)

AVERSE and ADVERSE

It is usual to say *averse from*, though there is good authority for *averse to*. But *adverse* is always *to*.

BACKGROUND

The Oxford English Dictionary recognises only two meanings for this word. One is " the ground or surface lying at the back of or beyond the chief objects of contemplation ". The other is " a less prominent position, where an object is not readily noticed ". The word has come into great favour, and is ranging a long way from the humble spheres assigned to it by the dictionary. Up to a point its extensions have been useful. To speak of examining the background of a proposal, in the sense of trying to find out what more there is in it than meets the eye, is a reasonable metaphor. And it is a reasonable extension of it to write:

> Men and women with widely divergent backgrounds, ranging from graduates and trained social workers to a coalminer, a railway clerk, and a clerk in an ironmongery store, had in fact succeeded.

But, like all these new favourites, it is beginning to get out of hand, and to displace more precise words:

> From your particulars it would appear that your background is more suitable for posts in Government Departments employing quantity surveyors.

This does not seem to mean anything different from " you are better qualified ".

It is surprising to find more women than men, but local experience provides the background ; during the war women left an area where there were no jobs for them.

Here it seems to be masquerading as *explanation.*

It was agreed that a warden should possess a sound educational background.

Here it falls under suspicion of doing nothing at all except show off. Why not " a sound education " ?

BACKLOG

The only meaning of *backlog* known to our dictionaries is a large log of wood forming the back of a fire on the hearth. But that is certainly not the meaning it is intended to convey in:

The most important step is to eliminate a very heavy backlog of orders on the manufacturers' books.

" Backlog " is perhaps more picturesque than " arrears " but it is not so intelligible, at any rate in this country. To us the G.P.O.'s " Waiting list of applicants " is clearer than the American Telephone Company's way of putting the same thing, " Backlog of held orders ".

BASIS

Basis, like *nature* and *character* and some other similar words, lures writers into roundabout ways. When you find you have written " on a . . . basis " always examine it critically before letting it stand.

Please state whether this is to be a permanent installation or on a temporary line basis. (Or a temporary line.)

If it is your intention to conduct the business arising from the use of these samples on the basis of manufacture for export. . . . (If the business arising from your use of these samples will be manufacture for export. . . .)

The issue of import licences on 100 per cent re-export basis. (The issue of import licences for re-export only.)

These will however remain Government property, being issued on a loan basis only. (Being issued on loan only.)

It has been found necessary to supply some markets on a ration basis. (To ration the supply to some markets.)

A legitimate use of *basis* is:

The manufacturers are distributing their products as fairly as possible on the basis of past trading.

BECAUSE

(i) *Because* preceded by *not* sometimes leads to ambiguity. " I did not write that letter because of what you told me " may mean either " I refrained from writing that letter because of what you told me " or " It was not because of what you told me that I wrote that letter ". Avoid this ambiguity by rewriting the sentence.

(ii) To say " the reason is . . . because " is to say " the reason is " twice over, since *because* is a conjunction that introduces a reason. You may say " I went because I was asked to go " or " the reason why I went was that I was asked to go ", but not " the reason why I went was because I was asked to go ".

See also NOT.

BEG

Never say " I beg to acknowledge " or " I beg to remain ", or use any phrase of that sort with *beg* in it. *Beg* in such a position can have no meaning. Its common use in this way is presumably to be accounted for by a false analogy with the reasonable use of *I beg* as a polite introduction to a contradiction, " I beg to differ ", or " I beg your leave to differ ". There is no reason why one should apologise, however faintly, for acknowledging a letter or remaining an obedient servant. *See* COMMERCIALESE.

BEG THE QUESTION

This does not mean, as is commonly supposed, to evade a straight answer to a question. It means to form a conclusion by making an assumption which is as much in need of proof as the conclusion itself. Logicians call this *petitio principii.* " Thus to say that parallel lines will never meet because they are parallel is simply to assume as a fact the very thing you profess to prove " (Brewer). A single word can be used in a question-begging way. *Reactionary*, *victimisation*, *aggression*, *imperialism* and *warmonger* are common examples.

BETWEEN

(i) *Between* and *among*. The O.E.D. tells us not to take too seriously those who tell us that *between* must only be used of two things and that when there are more the preposition must be *among*. It says :

Between is still the only word available to express the relation of a thing to many surrounding things severally and individually, *among* expressing a relationship to them collectively and vaguely: we should not say "the space lying among the three points", or "a treaty among three powers" or "the choice lies among the three candidates in the select list", or "to insert a needle among the closed petals of a flower".

(ii) *Between each.* Grammarians generally condemn the common use of *between* with *each* or *every*, as in "there will be a week's interval between each sitting". It is arguable that this can be justified as a convenient way of saying "between each sitting and the next", and that, considering how common it is, only pedantry can object. But those who want to be on the safe side will say either "weekly intervals between the sittings" or "a week's interval after each sitting".

(iii) *Between . . . or* and *between . . . and between.* If *between* is followed by a conjunction, this must always be a simple *and.* It is wrong to say: "the choice lies between Smith or Jones", or to say "we had to choose between taking these offices and making the best of them and between perhaps finding ourselves with no offices at all". If a sentence has become so involved that *and* is not felt to be enough it should be recast.

(iv) For *between you and I*, *see* I AND ME.

BILATERAL *see* UNILATERAL

BOTH

(i) When using *both . . . and*, be careful that these words are in their right positions and that each carries equal weight. Nothing that comes between the *both* and the *and* can be regarded as carried on after the *and.* If words are to be carried on after the *and* they must precede the *both* ; if they do not precede the *both* they must be repeated after the *and.* For instance:

He was both deaf to argument and entreaty.

Since *deaf to* comes after *both* it cannot be "understood" again after *and.* We must adjust the balance in one of the following ways:

He was both deaf to argument and unmoved by entreaty.

He was deaf both to argument and to entreaty.

He was deaf to both argument and entreaty.

(ii) Do not use *both* where it is not necessary because the meaning of the sentence is no less plain if you leave it cut:

Both of them are equally to blame. (They are equally to blame.)

Please ensure that both documents are fastened together. (. . . that the documents are fastened together.)

BOTTLENECK

Bottleneck is a useful and picturesque metaphor to denote the point of constriction of something that ought to be flowing freely:

> Even if the manufacturers could obtain ample raw material, the shortage of skilled labour would constitute a bottleneck in production.

The metaphor is not new, but it has recently had a sharp rise in popularity, perhaps because our economy has been so full of bottlenecks. It needs to be handled carefully in order to avoid absurdity: it is necessary to remember that the most troublesome bottleneck is not the biggest but the smallest.

BRACKETS

Be chary of using this word in its new-fangled sense of *class* or *category*. About this Ivor Brown says:

> The poor used to be called the poor; then they became, lest accuracy offend them, the under-privileged, or Lower Income Groups. Recently they have been called, especially by economists aiming at style, the Lower Income Brackets. I suppose the reference is to types and species bracketed together. But the usage is a stupid one. Somebody employed the term, I suppose, in an impressive article and so all the impressed readers decided to pay him the compliment of imitation.

See also GROUP.

For *brackets* in the usual sense, *see* PARENTHESIS.

BREAKDOWN

The ordinary writer should resist the popular novelty of using *breakdown* in a pseudo-scientific sense vaguely connoting analysis, subdivision, or classification of statistical matter. It is more than usually inept when used of things that can be physically broken down:

> The houses erected should be broken down into types. (classified according to type.)
>
> The breakdown of this number of houses into varying densities per acre. (division.)
>
> I should be glad if you would furnish a breakdown of all export orders on hand by countries of destination; only the total value of orders on hand received from each country is required. (a statement of the value of all the export orders you have on hand, showing the total for each country separately.)

Your export figures should be broken down between hard and soft currency areas. (given separately for.)

Averages are notoriously misleading, but even when the figures are broken down in detail, the general impression holds good. (even when the actual figures are examined.)

The Minister wishes to avoid fragmentation of the service by breaking down the two-tier system of administration provided for in the Act into a three-tier system.

Why *breaking down* in the last example ? If the word *break* must be used at all *breaking up* would go better with *fragmentation.* But why not some ordinary word such as *changing*, *altering* or *converting ?*

The fascination of this word may lead government departments into the ludicrous:

Care should be taken that the breakdown of patients by the department under whose care they were immediately before discharge is strictly followed. (*Classification* is presumably meant.)

BUT

(i) *But*, in the sense of *except* is a preposition and takes the objective case. So it is not ungrammatical to say " Nobody but him attended the meeting ". But it is more usual to treat *but* in that position as a conjunction and say: " Nobody but he attended the meeting ".

(ii) In using *but* as a conjunction an easy slip is to put it where there should be an *and*, forgetting that the conjunction that you want is one that does not go contrary to the clause immediately preceding but continues in the same sense.

It is agreed that the primary condition of the scheme is satisfied, but it is also necessary to establish that your war service interrupted an organised course of study for a professional qualification comparable to that for which application is made, *but* as explained in previous letters you are unable to fulfil this condition.

The italicised *but* should be *and.* The line of thought has already been turned by the first *but* ; it is now going straight on.

A similar slip is made in :

The Forestry Commission will probably only be able to offer you a post as a Forest Labourer, or possibly in leading a gang of forest workers, but there are at the moment no vacancies for Forest Officers.

Either *only* must be omitted or the *but* must be changed to *since.*

(iii) There is no ground for the idea that it is incorrect to begin a sentence with *but* or *and.* *See* AND.

CALCULATED *see* LIKELY

CAPABLE

> Both these young men feel that they would be capable to undertake the work.

This is wrong. We say " able to undertake ", but it must be " capable of undertaking ". *See* ING ENDINGS, para. (v).

CASE

The sins of this word are well known ; it has been said that there is perhaps no single word so freely resorted to as a trouble-saver and consequently responsible for so much flabby writing.

Here are some examples to show how what might be a simple and straightforward statement becomes enmeshed in the coils of phrases formed with *case:*

> The cost of maintenance of the building would be higher than was the case with a building of traditional construction. (The cost of maintenance of the building would be higher than that of a building of traditional construction.)
>
> That country is not now so short of sterling as was formerly the case. (As it used to be.)
>
> Since the officiating president in the case of each major institute takes up his office on widely differing dates. (Since the officiating presidents of the major institutes take up office on widely differing dates.)
>
> The National Coal Board is an unwieldy organisation, in many cases quite out of touch with the coalfields.

It is not easy to guess the meaning of this last example.

This trick-use of *case* is even worse when the reader might be misled, if only momentarily, into thinking that a physical case was meant :

> Cases have thus arisen in which goods have been exported without the knowledge of this Commission.
>
> Water for domestic use is carried by hand in many cases from road standpipes.

There are, of course, many legitimate uses of the word, and writers should not be frightened away from it altogether by Quiller-Couch's much-quoted and rather overdone onslaught. There are for instance (to borrow from Fowler) :

> A case of measles.
> You have no case.
> In case of need, or fire, or other emergency.
> A case of burglary or other crime.
> A law case of any sort.
> Circumstances alter cases.

But do not say " that is not the case " when you mean " that is not so ", or " It is not the case that I wrote that letter ", when you mean " It is not true that I wrote that letter ", or merely " I did not write that letter ".

CEILING

Ceiling is one of the bright young metaphors that are now so fashionable, and are displacing the old fogeys. *Ceiling's* victims are *maximum* and *limit*. There is no great harm in that, so long as those who use the word remember to treat it as a metaphor. *See* METAPHOR.

> The advisory Committee did not apply for a general increase in the ceilings.

Ceilings here means *maximum prices*. The writer forgot that if one wants more headroom one does not increase the ceiling; one raises it. Similarly anyone who thinks that " within the monetary licensing ceiling " is the most effective way of expressing his meaning (though I cannot believe it really is) ought at least to remember that our normal relationship to a ceiling is under it, not within it.

> In determining the floor-space, a ceiling of 15,000 square feet should normally be the limit.

This is indeed a complicated way of saying that floor-space should not normally exceed 15,000 square feet. Why drag down the ceiling?

When this metaphor, not content with swallowing *maximum*, tries to absorb *minimum* too, we pass from the tolerable to the grotesque:

> The effect of this announcement is that the total figure for 1950/51 of £410 million can be regarded as a floor as well as a ceiling.

CHANGES IN THE MEANING OF WORDS

Words change their meaning, sometimes usefully, sometimes not. It is proper to struggle against a changing meaning when the change does not enrich the language but merely blunts a fine edge. This book contains several protests against changes of this sort, for instance the encroachment of *alibi* on *excuse*, of *anticipate* on *expect*, of *claim* on *assert*, of *following* on *after* and of *due to* on *owing to*.

But it is not reasonable to condemn the use of a word in a well-established sense merely because its etymological meaning is different:

> To hold us to the bald etymology is a pedantry of the plain man, or of the half-educated man, who has not regarded its growth. . . . The word *apostate* for example means for us far more than an *absentee*

or a *dissenter*, and a *muscle* more than a little mouse ; *monks* rarely live alone ; your *anecdote* is anything but clandestine ; *rivals* contend for other than water rights, and *hypocrites* are no longer confined to the theatre. (Sir Clifford Allbutt : *Notes on the composition of scientific papers*, Macmillan 1925.)

CHARACTER

Beware of the roundabout phrases formed with this and similar words (*nature*, for instance) and used instead of simple adjectives:

An undertaking of a hazardous character (hazardous undertaking).

The weather will be of a showery character (it will be showery).

Industrialists of a more substantial character (more substantial industrialists).

Work of maintenance and repair of a less urgent character (less urgent work of maintenance and repair).

CIRCUMSTANCES

It used to be widely held by people with a little learning that to say " under the circumstances " must be wrong because what is around us cannot be over us. " In the circumstances " was the only correct expression. This argument is characterised by Fowler as puerile. Its major premiss is not true (" a threatening sky is a circumstance no less than a threatening bulldog ") and even if it were true it would be irrelevant, because, as cannot be too often repeated, English idiom has a contempt for logic. There is good authority for *under the circumstances*, and if some of us prefer *in the circumstances* (as I do), that is a matter of taste, not of rule.

CLAIM

The dictionary meaning of *to claim* is " to demand as one's own, to assert and demand the recognition of a right ". " In the U.S.A. loosely ", adds the dictionary, " it is used in the sense of to assert or to allege ".

This " loose " usage is no longer confined to the U.S.A. Here are some recent examples from this country:

The police took statements from about forty people who claimed that they had seen the gunmen in different parts of the city.

The State Department claims that discrimination is being shown against the American Film Industry.

There are those who claim that the Atlantic Treaty has an aggressive purpose.

> I have a friend who claims to keep in his office a filing tray labelled "Too Difficult."

This use has become so common, and is found in such respectable places, that the fight against it should probably be regarded as lost. That will be deplored by all those who like to treat words as tools of precision, and to keep their edges sharp. Why should *claim*, which has its own useful job to do, claim a job that is already being efficiently done by others? Perhaps the idea underlying this usage is that the writer claims credence for an improbable assertion.

CLICHÉ

Fowler's definition of a cliché is:

> A French name for such hackneyed phrases as, not being the simple or natural way of expressing what is to be expressed, have served when first used as real improvements on that in some particular context, but have acquired an unfortunate popularity and come into general use even when they are not more but less suitable to the context than plain speech.

This definition may be rounded off by Eric Partridge's comment:

> They range from fly-blown phrases (explore every avenue) through sobriquets that have lost all point and freshness (the Iron Duke) to quotations that have become debased currency (cups that cheer but not inebriate), metaphors that are now pointless, and formulas that have become mere counters (far be it from me to . . .).

A cliché then is by definition a bad thing, not to be employed by self-respecting writers. Judged by this test, some expressions are unquestionably and in all circumstances clichés. This is true in particular of verbose and facetious ways of saying simple things (*conspicuous by its absence*, *tender mercies*, *durance vile*) and of phrases so threadbare that they cannot escape the suspicion of being used automatically (*leave no stone unturned*, *acid test*, *psychological moment*, *leave severely alone*). But a vast number of other expressions may or may not be clichés. It depends on whether they are used unthinkingly as reach-me-downs or deliberately chosen as the best means of saying what the writer wants to say. Eric Partridge's Dictionary of Clichés contains some thousands of entries. But, as he says in his preface, what is a cliché is partly a matter of opinion. It is also a matter of occasion. Many of those in his dictionary may or may not be clichés; it depends on how they are used. Examples are: to *cross the Rubicon*, to *cry over spilt milk*, *a work of supererogation* and to *break the ice*. Such phrases as these may be the fittest way of expressing a writer's meaning. If you choose one for that reason, and not because you think it fine, or because it is the first thing that came into your head, you need not be afraid of being called a cliché-monger.

COLLECTIVE WORDS

In using collective words or nouns of multitude (*Department*, *Parliament*, *Government*, *Committee* and the like), ought we to say " the Government have decided " or " the Government has decided "; " the Committee are meeting ", or " the Committee is meeting "? There is no rule; either a singular or plural verb may be used. It is true that some grammarians advise the plural when the emphasis is on the individual members and the singular when it is on the body as a whole. But that seems over-nice, and the official may be content with making sure that one or the other is followed consistently in the same document. Failure to do this is a common form of carelessness:

> The firm *has* given an undertaking that in the event of *their* having to restrict production . . .
>
> The industry *is* capable of supplying all home requirements and *have* in fact been exporting.
>
> It will be for each committee to determine in the light of *its* responsibilities how far it is necessary to make all these appointments, and no appointment should be made unless the committee *are* fully satisfied of the need.

It is on the whole safer to use the plural, if only because the singular may lead to difficulty when the pronoun has to be used. *They* think, of a Committee, sounds more natural than *it* thinks.

Do not forget to make your relative pronoun correspond. If you use the singular the relative must be *which*, if the plural it must be *who*.

COLLUSION

Collusion always implies dirty work. If the enterprise is innocent, *collaboration* or *co-operation* should be used.

COLON

Opinions vary about the proper uses of the colon in punctuation.

As one of a series of stops ranging in strength from the comma to the full-stop, it has gone out of fashion with the " period " style of writing. Its main functions are now:

(*a*) Between two sentences in antithesis:

> Man proposes: God disposes.

(*b*) To precede an explanation or particularisation, in the same way that the dash may be used; in the words of Fowler "to deliver the goods that have been invoiced in the preceding words":

> News reaches a national paper from two sources: the news agencies and its own correspondents.

For the second purpose the dash is the colon's weaker relative. *See* DASH.

COMMA

The use of commas cannot be learned by rule. Not only does conventional practice vary from period to period, but good writers of the same period differ among themselves. Moreover stops have two kinds of duty. One is to show the construction of sentences—the "grammatical" duty. The other is to introduce nuances into the meaning—the "rhetorical" duty. "I went to his house and I found him there" is a colourless statement. "I went to his house, and I found him there" hints that it was not quite a matter of course that he should have been found there. "I went to his house. And I found him there". This indicates that to find him there was surprising. Similarly you can give a different nuance to what you write by encasing adverbs or adverbial phrases in commas. "He was, apparently, willing to support you" throws a shade of doubt on his bona fides that is not present in "He was apparently willing to support you".

The correct use of the comma—if there is such a thing as "correct" use—can only be acquired by commonsense, observation and taste. The best general advice is Fowler's:

> Everyone should make up his mind not to depend on his stops. . . . It may almost be said that what reads wrongly if the stops are removed is radically bad: stops are not to alter the meaning but merely to show it up.

Difficult though it may be to describe the correct uses of the comma, there is general agreement among the authorities that certain uses are incorrect. A warning can usefully be given against the commonest of these. Here are some of them.

(i) The use of a comma between two independent sentences not linked by a conjunction. A heavier stop should always be used in this position, usually a semicolon:

> We wrote on the 12th May asking for an urgent report regarding the above contractor's complaint, this was followed up on the 24th May by a telephone call.
>
> You may not be aware that a Youth Employment Service is operating throughout the country, in some areas it is under the

control of the Ministry of Labour and National Service and in others of the Education Authorities.

There should be a semicolon after *complaint* in the first quotation and *country* in the second.

> The Department cannot guarantee that a licence will be issued, you should not therefore arrange for any shipment.

> I regret the delay in replying to your letter but Mr. X who was dealing with it is on leave, however, I have gone into the matter. . . .

There should be a full stop after *issued* in the first quotation and after *leave* in the second.

(ii) The use of a comma to mark the end of the subject of a verb, or the beginning of the object. *See* ARRANGEMENT.

It cannot be said to be always wrong to use a comma to mark the end of a composite subject, because good writers sometimes do it deliberately. For instance one might write:

> The question whether it is legitimate to use a comma to mark the end of the subject, is an arguable one.

But the comma is unnecessary; the reader does not need its help. To use commas in this way is a dangerous habit; it encourages a writer to shirk the trouble of so arranging his sentences as to make their meaning plain without punctuation.

> I am however to draw your attention to the fact that goods subject to import licensing which are despatched to this country without the necessary licence having first been obtained, are on arrival liable to seizure. . . .

If the subject is felt to be so long that it needs a boundary post at the end, it would be better not to use the slovenly device of a comma but to rewrite the sentence in conditional form.

> . . . if goods subject to import licensing are despatched . . . they are on arrival . . .

Postponement of the object may get a writer into the same sort of trouble.

> In the case of both whole-time and part-time officers, the general duties undertaken by them include the duty of treating without any additional remuneration and without any right to recover private fees, patients in their charge who are occupying Section 5 accommodation under the proviso to Section 5 (1) of the Act.

This unlovely sentence obviously needs recasting. One way of doing this would be:

> The general duties undertaken by both whole-time and part-time officers include the treating of patients in their charge who are occupying Section 5 accommodation under the proviso to Section 5 (1) of the Act, and they are not entitled to any additional remuneration for it or to recover private fees.

(iii) The use of one comma instead of either a pair or none.

This very common blunder is more easily illustrated than explained:

> Against all this must be set considerations which, in our submission are overwhelming. (Omit the comma.)
>
> We should be glad if you would inform us for our record purposes, of any agency agreement finally reached. (Either omit the comma or insert one after *us*.)
>
> It will be noted that for the development areas, Treasury-financed projects are to be grouped together. (Either omit the comma or insert one after *that*.)
>
> The first is the acute shortage that so frequently exists, of suitable premises where people can come together. (Either omit the comma or insert one after *shortage*.)
>
> The principal purpose is to provide for the division between the minister and the governing body concerned, of premises and property held partly for hospital purposes and partly for other purposes. (Omit the comma.)

(iv) The use of commas with " defining " relative clauses.

Relative clauses fall into two main classes. Grammarians give them different labels, but *defining* and *commenting* are the most convenient and descriptive. If you say " The man who was here this morning told me that ", the relative clause is a defining one; it completes the subject " the man ", which conveys no definite meaning without it. But if you say: " Jones, who was here this morning, told me that ", the relative clause is commenting; the subject " Jones " is already complete and the relative clause merely adds a bit of information about him which may or may not be important but is not essential to the definition of the subject. A commenting clause should be within commas; a defining one should not. This is not an arbitrary rule; it is a utilitarian one. If you do not observe it, you may fail to make your meaning clear, or you may even say something different from what you intend. For instance:

> I have to express regret for the error which occurred in printing.

By not putting a comma after *error* the writer has made the relative clause a defining one. He implies that he regrets the error that occurred in printing, but has no regrets about any errors that occurred in other ways. That is not what he wanted to say. Both he and his correspondent know what the error is that they are writing about. It does not need defining. What the writer of the letter wants to do is to express his regret and to say that it is the printer's fault. To do this he must put a comma after error, and make the relative clause a commenting one.

Here is an example of the opposite mistake:

> I have made enquiries, and find that the clerk, who dealt with your enquiry, recorded the name of the firm incorrectly.

The relative clause here is a defining one. The comma turns it into a commenting one and implies that the writer has only one clerk. The truth is that one of several is being singled out; and this is made clear if the commas after *clerk* and *enquiry* are omitted.

The same mistake is made in:

> The Ministry issues permits to employing authorities to enable foreigners to land in this country for the purpose of taking up employment, for which British subjects are not available.

The grammatical implication of this is that employment in general is not a thing for which British subjects are available.

An instruction book called " Pre-aircrew English " supplied during the war to airmen in training in one of the Dominions, contained an encouragement to its readers to " smarten up their English ". This ended:

> Pilots, whose minds are dull, do not usually live long.

The commas convert a truism into an insult.

(v) The insertion of a meaningless comma into an " absolute phrase ".

An absolute phrase (e.g. " then, the work being finished, we went home ") always has commas round it. But there is no sense in the comma that so often carelessly appears inside it.

> The House of Commons, having passed the third reading by a large majority after an animated debate, the bill was sent to the Lords.

The insertion of the first comma leaves the House of Commons in the air waiting for a verb that never comes. *See* ING ENDINGS.

A comma was at one time always used to introduce *that* clauses.

> It is a just though trite observation, that victorious Rome was itself subdued by the arts of Greece. (Gibbon.)

> The true meaning is so uncertain and remote, that it is never sought. (Johnson.)

> The author well knew, that two gentlemen . . . had differed with him. (Burke.)

We are more sparing of commas nowadays, and this practice has gone out of fashion, though some good writers still put commas in that position occasionally.

As to the legitimate uses of commas, it is unprofitable, for the reasons explained, to try to enumerate them: they can best be learned by observation. But there are a few points on which some guidance may be useful:

(i) Words and phrases in series.

In such a sentence as:

> The company included Ambassadors, Ministers, Bishops and Judges

commas are always put after each item in the series up to the last but one, but practice varies about putting a comma between the last but one and the *and* introducing the last. Neither practice is wrong. Those who favour a comma (a minority, but gaining ground) argue that, since a comma may sometimes be necessary to prevent ambiguity, there had better be one there always. Supposing the sentence were:

> The company included the Bishops of Winchester, Salisbury, Bristol, and Bath and Wells

the reader unversed in the English ecclesiastical hierarchy needs the comma after *Bristol* in order to sort out the last two bishops. Without it they might be, grammatically and geographically, either (a) Bristol and Bath and (b) Wells, or (a) Bristol and (b) Bath and Wells. Ambiguity cannot be justified by saying that those who are interested will know what is meant and those who are not will not care.

Where the series is of adjectives preceding a noun, it is a matter of taste whether there are commas between them or not:

> A silly verbose pompous letter, and
> A silly, verbose, pompous letter

are equally correct. The commas merely give a little emphasis to the adjectives. Where the final adjective is one that describes the species of the noun, it must of course be regarded as part of the noun, and not be preceded by a comma. Thus:

> A silly, verbose, pompous official letter.

(ii) Commas for emphasis or clarity.

Commas in pairs give a parenthetic effect to what they enclose which may vary from a true parenthesis (" These things, our correspondent says, have caused widespread discontent ") or an explanation in apposition (" Mr. Jones, the Secretary, said . . . ") to the emphasising of an adverb or adverbial phrase:

> The amendment was, fortunately, ruled out of order.
> We may, some day, get a decision.

The notes of relief in the first and of hopelessness in the second are emphasised by the commas.

Or the effect of commas may be to emphasise the subject of the sentence " He, however, thought differently ". The commas underline *he*.

Except for emphasis, or sometimes for clarity, it is better not to comma-off adverbs and adverbial phrases. Many writers and more compositors and typists habitually so treat such words as *however*, *moreover*, *therefore*, *indeed*, *of course*, *no doubt*, *perhaps*, and even *also* and *too*. Not only is this unnecessary but it throws away a convenient means of adding emphasis when emphasis is needed.

Commas are sometimes needed to prevent ambiguity by showing what an adverb qualifies. *However* is a word that is specially likely to lead a reader astray. For instance, Burke writes:

> The author is compelled, however reluctantly, to receive the sentence pronounced on him in the House of Commons as that of the Party.

The meaning of this sentence would be different if the comma after *reluctantly* were omitted, and one inserted after *however*.

> The author is compelled, however, reluctantly to receive, etc.

Other adverbs may need similar clarification. This example is taken from Lord Dunsany:

> I am going to Dublin perhaps, with Murphy,

which does not mean the same as

> I am going to Dublin, perhaps with Murphy.

Adverbs and adverbial phrases standing at the beginning of sentences are often given superfluous commas:

> In their absence, it will be desirable . . .
>
> Nevertheless, there is need for special care . . .
>
> In practice, it has been found advisable . . .

Those commas cannot be said to be wrong; the use of commas in this way is frequent in good writing. But they are unnecessary, and therefore we are better without them unless they are needed to prevent the reader from going off on a wrong scent, as in:

> A few days after, the Minister of Labour promised that a dossier of the strike would be published.
>
> Two miles on, the road is worse.

(iii) Other uses to prevent ambiguity.

Ambiguities of various kinds, besides those already mentioned, can often be removed by punctuation. Sometimes this is legitimate, sometimes not. The writer must not forget Fowler's dictum: " It may almost be said that what reads wrongly if the stops are removed is radically bad ". He should consider whether the comma is felt to be naturally placed or to be logically intrusive. Apart from the uses already referred to in marking where the subject ends and the predicate begins (generally illegitimate) and in showing what an adverb qualifies (generally legitimate) the most common use of the comma as a clarifier is to show that what follows it refers not to what immediately precedes it but to something further back. William Cobbett, in the grammar that he wrote for his young son, pointed out that "You will be rich if you be industrious, in a few years" did not mean the same as "you will be rich, if you be industrious in a few years". The comma that precedes the adverbial phrase *in a few years* indicates that that phrase refers not to "if you be industrious" but to the whole clause "you will be rich if you be industrious". As usual, the device is clumsy. The proper way of writing the sentence is "You will be rich in a few years if you be industrious". Arrange your words in the right order and you will not need these artificial aids.

COMMENCE

Commence is described by the O.E.D. as "more formal than begin". *Begin* should therefore be preferred for all ordinary purposes.

COMMERCIALESE

Public opinion today generally endorses the verdict of the Departmental Committee on the Teaching of English in England (1921):

> We have no hesitation in reporting that Commercial English is not only objectionable to all those who have the purity of the language at heart, but also contrary to the true interests of commercial life, sapping its vitality and encouraging the use of dry, meaningless, formulae just where vigorous and arresting English is the chief requisite.

The Committee added this footnote:

> Some readers of the Report may be unacquainted with "commercial English". We therefore give a few examples of the words and idiom in the dialect:— *prox* (next month); *ult* (last month); *of even date* (of today); *beg to* or *hereby beg to* (a meaningless prefix, found before verbs of all kinds, e.g. "I beg to inform you" "hereby beg to say" etc.); *Your favour, Your esteemed favour, yours* (your letter); *I am in receipt of your favour, Your favour duly to hand*, or, more familiarly, *Yours to hand* (Your letter has reached me); *per* (by); *as per* (in accordance with); *same* (it, e.g. "Yours to hand and we beg to say we shall give all attention to same"); *make or quote you* (make you an offer, e.g. "We can make you a discount of 6 per cent", "My traveller had the pleasure of quoting you for the order"); *The favour of your immediate reply will oblige* (I shall be glad to hear from you at once).

To these might be added *Please find*, *Thanking you in anticipation*, the use of *item* to mean anything the writer pleases (*see* ITEM) and that curious piece of tortuous politeness *Your good self.*

COMPARATIVELY *see* RELATIVELY and COMPARATIVELY (and UNDULY)

COMPARE

There is a difference between *compare to* and *compare with* ; the first is to liken one thing to another; the second is to note the resemblances and differences between two things. Thus:

> Shall I compare thee to a Summer's day?
>
> If we compare the speaker's notes with the report of his speech in *The Times* . . .

COMPRISE and COMPOSE

These words are often confused especially by the use of *comprise* for *compose.* A body comprises (or consists of) the elements of which it is composed (or constituted) ; in the first example, for instance, Op. 77 comprises the quartettes, not the other way round. *Compose* or *constitute* or *form* should have been used in all examples.

> The two quartettes comprising Handel's Op. 77.
>
> The smaller Regional Hospitals which comprise a large proportion of those available to Regional Boards.
>
> The twelve Foreign Ministers who comprise the Atlantic Treaty Council.

CONCERNED (SO FAR AS . . . IS CONCERNED)

A correspondent has written asking me to:

> scarify the phrase " so far as . . . is concerned ", e.g. " the war is over so far as Germany is concerned ", an actual instance ; or " so far as he was concerned interest in the game was over ". After long and vigilant watch I have still to find a case in which a single preposition would not be clearer as well as shorter. I suspect that my fellow-journalists are more addicted to this use of the phrase than civil servants; but these are not guiltless.

I would gladly do so, but I have been forestalled by Professor Kapp, who devotes to this useful task a large part of Chapter X (" Circumlocutions ") of his book *The Presentation of Technical Information* (Constable 1948). I could not improve on his scarification; and to condense it would be to spoil it.

It is perhaps putting the case too high to say that " so far as . . . concerned " could always be replaced by a single preposition. I do not think that the phrase can be dispensed with by those who wish to emphasise that they have blinkers on, and are concerned only with one aspect of a question. " So far as I am concerned you may go home " implies that someone else has a say too. Or again:

> So far as the provisions of the Trading with the Enemy Act are concerned, the sum so released may . . . be utilized to reimburse you for expenses. . . .

There is no other equally convenient way of making clear that the writer is removing only the impediment created by the Act and is not concerned with any other impediment there may be.

Possibly, though less certainly, this sentence might claim the same indulgence :

> The effect of the suggested system, so far as the pharmaceutical industry is concerned, would be to ensure rewards for research and development work until the new preparations were absorbed into the B.P.

It might be argued that we should not get quite the same meaning from " on the pharmaceutical industry " ; this destroys the suggestion that there may be other effects, but the writer is not concerning himself with them.

But these are exceptions. There is no doubt that the phrase is generally a cloak for muddled thinking:

> The ruling factor, so far as native trade is concerned, is price. (The ruling factor in native trade is price.)
>
> Some were opposed to hanging as a means of execution where women were concerned. (As a means of executing women.)
>
> There has been no material change so far as the drafting of a formal application is concerned. (There has been no material change ; no formal application has yet been drafted.)
>
> Wood pulp manufacture on a commercial scale is a very recent development so far as time is concerned. (Omit the last six words.)

CONFIRM

The natural meaning of to *confirm* is to *support* or *corroborate*: " Will you please confirm your secretary's telephone message." By extension it is sometimes wrongly used as if it meant *say* or *tell me*: " Will you please confirm whether you have received my cheque." It is commoner in commercialese than in officialese e.g. " Please confirm voltage and whether AC or DC " in which it apparently means merely " let me know ".

CONNEXION (IN THIS CONNEXION)

Though *connection* is common, *connexion* is the correct spelling.

The phrase " in this connexion " (which has its proper uses) is one of the commonest forms of " padding " in official writing.

See PADDING. In all the following examples the words should be omitted; they are doing no work.

> I am directed to refer to the travelling and subsistence allowances applicable to your Department, and in this connexion I am to say . . .
>
> Mr. X is an applicant for appointment as a clerk in this Department and in this connexion I shall be glad if you will complete the attached form.
>
> The Minister's views in general in this connexion and the nature and scope of the information which he felt would assist him in this connexion was indicated at a meeting . . .

On the use of the singular verb *was*, *see* SINGULAR and PLURAL VERBS.

> You will recollect that you anticipated despatching the material in three stages, i.e. April, May and during the first half of the present month. In this connexion I shall be glad of your confirmation that the April and May deliveries were maintained.

On this use of *anticipated*, *see* ANTICIPATE.

> It is noted that you wish to apply for . . . and in this connexion I have to advise you to contact . . .

On the use of *contact*, *see* CONTACT.

CONSEQUENT and CONSEQUENTIAL

Consequential has now only two meanings in common use. It retains that of *self-important*, and in legal language it signifies a secondary and incidental result, especially in the phrases *consequential damages* and *consequential amendments*. These latter are formal amendments made necessary by the carrying of some other amendment. For all other purposes *consequent* is the adjective of *consequence*. Thus a Minister might say " This amendment is consequent on a promise I gave on second reading " and " This amendment is consequential on one accepted yesterday ".

CONSIDERABLE

Do not use this adjective without being sure that it is the one you want. *See* ADJECTIVES.

> A programme of this magnitude will necessarily take a considerable period to complete.

Is " a considerable period " the same as " a long time " ? If so, the plain words are better.

CONSIDERATION (UNDER CONSIDERATION)

This phrase has become a cliché. *See* CLICHÉ. For this reason it has been necessary to invent the expression " under active consideration ", which is itself on the way to becoming a cliché. It is an old civil service joke that " The matter is under consideration " means " We have lost the file ", and " The matter is under active consideration " means " We are trying to find the file ". These expressions should be avoided if possible, though it may sometimes be difficult to do without them.

CONSTITUTE

Do not use the verb *to constitute* if the verb *to be* will do.

> It was decided that these considerations did not constitute a fatal objection (were not a fatal objection).

CONSIST

There is a difference between *consist of* and *consist in*. *Consist of* denotes the substance of which the subject is made ; *consist in* defines the subject.

> The writing desks consist of planks on trestles.
> The work of the branch consists in interviewing the public.

CONTACT *see* NEW VERBS

If *contact* is to be admitted as a verb, its justification must be, as Ivor Brown has said, that " there is no word which covers approach by telephone, letter and speech, and *contact* is self-explanatory and concise ". The " contact-man ", we may be sure, needs a word to describe him which will include every conceivable method of approach.

It is therefore pointless to write " It would be appreciated if you would either write or contact this office ". The words " either write or " are superfluous. *Contact* as a verb can only be allowed to live if it saves us the trouble of saying " write or telephone or call ". Even so it excites such violent antipathy in some people that it is better to avoid it for the present and to write *get into touch with* instead.

CONTINUAL and CONTINUOUS

Continuous means without intermission. *Continual* means frequently recurring. " It rained continually all day " means that it never left off for long. " It rained continuously all day " means that it never left off at all.

COURSE (OF COURSE)

Unconscious iteration of this phrase is a common trick. It may be presumed that there is more than one reason for this. One, which affects journalists more than officials, is that the writer wants to show off. When Macaulay says that every schoolboy knows something that most of us have never heard of, we are impressed by the omniscience of a writer to whom such things are a commonplace of the school-room. In the same way a journalist may use *of course* to impress his readers by showing his familiarity with an out of the way piece of information or with great personages, a temptation to which gossip-writers seem specially susceptible.

But the official is more likely to overwork *of course* from genuine humility. He puts it in so as not to seem didactic: "don't think that I suppose you to be so stupid that you don't already know or infer what I am telling you, but I think I ought to mention it". Sometimes *of course* is wisely used for this purpose—if for instance the writer has good reason to say something so obvious as to make a touchy reader feel that he is being treated like a fool. It is better in such circumstances to say "of course" than its pompous variant "as you are no doubt aware". But the danger of using *of course* too often is greater than that of using it too seldom.

DASH

The dash has several legitimate uses, though not so many as are ascribed to it by those who treat it as a labour-saving device that spares them the trouble of thinking of the right stop. On account of this seductive property it should be employed with discretion. The following recognised usages are probably enough for all ordinary purposes, and it will be wise not to go outside them.

(i) In pairs for a parenthesis. *See* PARENTHESIS.

(ii) To introduce a correction, amplification, or explanation of what immediately precedes it:

> The National Joint Council consists of 22 members—11 appointed by each side.
>
> The plan is concerned with the situation some ten to fifteen years ahead—say about 1960.

(iii) To gather together a composite subject before passing to the predicate:

> The severely crippled, the social misfit, the mentally unstable—all have found their way into the public assistance institution.

(iv) With a colon to introduce a substantial quotation or a list (e.g. *as follows:—*). This, though common, is unnecessary since either the colon or the dash can do all that is needed by itself.

DATA

Data, unlike *agenda*, remains the plural word that it is in Latin.

> Unless firm data is available at an early date . . .

This is wrong. *Is* should be *are*.

If a singular is wanted, it is usually *one of the data*, not *datum*. The ordinary meaning of *datum* is :

> Any position or element in relation to which others are determined : chiefly in the phrases : *datum point*, a point assumed or used as a basis of reckoning, adjustment or the like—*datum line* a horizontal line from which heights and depths of points are reckoned, as in a railroad plan. . . . (Webster.)

DE and DIS

Each of these is termed by the O.E.D. " a living prefix with privative force ". " Living " is the right word ; they have been living riotously of late. Anyone, it seems, can make a new verb by prefixing *de* to an existing one. Some years ago Sir Alan Herbert made a collection of some remarkable recent creations of this sort, and included them in his *index expurgatorius* of " septic verbs ". Among them were *debureaucratise*, *decontaminate*, *dedirt*, *dehumidify*, *deinsectize*, *deratizate*, *derestrict*, *dewater*, *dezincify*. *Derequisition* was not there; it must have been a later creation.

Some of these, it is to be hoped, may prove to be freaks of an occasion and will be seen no more. But there is a class which has come to stay, whether we like it or not. This comprises *decontaminate*, *derestrict*, and *derequisition*. Their origin is the same : they all denote the undoing of something the doing of which called for—or at any rate was given—a special term. If to affect with gas is to *contaminate*, to enforce a speed limit is to *restrict*, and to commandeer a house is to *requisition* then the cancellation of those things will inevitably be *decontaminate*, *derestrict*, and *derequisition*, whether we like it or not, and it is no use saying that they ought to be *cleanse*, *exempt* and *release*, or any other words that are not directly linked with their opposites.

As to *dis*, the word that moved Sir Alan Herbert most, at the time when he was writing, was *disequilibrium*. Today the favourites are *disincentive* and *disinflation*. *Incentive* has become almost a term of art in political economy, and *inflation* has long been one. Both are much on our lips just now. They have their established opposites, says the purist, *deterrent* and *deflation*. But do these really mean quite the same as *disincentive* and *disinflation* ? If the answer is—as it seems to be—that we need special words for that particular from of deterrent that discourages men from working hard, and for that process of checking inflation which is something less than deflation, we may as well give in. But what is alarming is that those who go in for the invention of opposites by means of "living prefixes with privative force" do not know when to stop. It becomes a disease. *Disincentive* replaces *deterrent*; then *undisincentive* ousts *incentive*, and then *disincentive* itself has to yield to *non-undisincentive*. No wonder Mr. G. V. Carey is moved to write to *The Times*:

> I have long been waiting for somebody to dispel my growing bewilderment at the modern expression of affirmative and negative (or should I say "disaffirmative"?) in English. I had always imagined that the opposite of "harmony" was "discord", not "disharmony"; of "incentive", "deterrent"; and so on. But at the present rate of distortion of our language it looks as though we shall soon be talking about "black and disblack", "good and disgood".

In the "newspeak" which George Orwell pictured as the language of 1984 *very bad* has become *doubleplusungood*.

See also New Verbs, Non *and* Un.

DEADLINE

The dictionary meaning of deadline is a "line drawn round a military prison beyond which a prisoner may be shot down". By a natural and useful extension it has taken on the meaning of any line beyond which it is not permitted or possible to go, and so, in general, a line of demarcation, especially between the safe and the unsafe. But, like all picturesque novelties of the vocabulary, it is showing a roving disposition that needs to be curbed. Of a threatened bus strike on a Saturday afternoon we were told:

> Many shops sent their employees away at quarter-hour intervals during the morning, so that they could avoid the one o'clock deadline for the strike.

In telling news the simple way is generally the best way, and the simple thing that had to be said was that the employees were sent away early so that they could be home before the strike began at one o'clock. We have no need of a new word for *starting-time*.

DEARTH *see* Lack

DECIMATE

To *decimate* is to reduce *by* one-tenth, not *to* one-tenth. It meant originally to punish mutinous troops by executing one man in ten, chosen by lot. Hence by extension it means to destroy a large proportion; the suggestion it now conveys is usually of a loss much greater than ten per cent. Because of the flavour of exactness that still hangs about it, an adverb or adverbial phrase should never be used with it. We may say "The attacking troops were decimated", meaning that they suffered heavy losses, but we must not say "The attacking troops were badly decimated", and still less "decimated to the extent of fifty per cent. or more".

The following truly remarkable instance of the misuse of *decimate* was given in the course of correspondence in *The Times* about the misuse of *literally*. *See* LITERALLY.

> I submit the following, long and lovingly remembered from my "penny dreadful" days: "Dick, hotly pursued by the scalp-hunter, turned in his saddle, fired, and literally decimated his opponent".

DEEM

This is an old-fashioned word which starches any letter in which it is used as a synonym for *think*. But it is still useful in its technical sense of signifying the constructive or inferential as opposed to the explicit or actual. "Everyone is deemed to have intended the natural and probable consequences of his actions": "anyone who does not give notice of objection within three weeks will be deemed to have agreed": "any expenditure incurred in the preparation of plans for any work . . . shall be deemed to be included in the expenditure incurred in carrying out that work."

> Almost every Act of Parliament bids us deem something to be what it plainly is not. (Lord Macmillan in *The Sunday Times*, 14th August, 1949.)

DEFECTIVE and DEFICIENT

Defective is associated with *defect*, and *deficient* with *deficit*. (Fowler.) It follows that *defective* is appropriate primarily to what is wanting in quality, and *deficient* to what is wanting in quantity. That is a sound rule to follow, but it does not always give clear guidance, because it is not always clear whether what is wrong is a defect or a deficiency. Illumination may be bad because the lamps are poor in quality or because they are insufficient in quantity, and we may not know whether to call it *deficient* or *defective*. Someone who is "not all there" may be in that unfortunate state either because (as the expression suggests) his brains are insufficient in quantity or because they are below the standard quality. So we may call him indifferently either mentally defective or mentally deficient. But where the distinction is clear, in the interests of clarity of thought it should be preserved.

DEFINITE and DEFINITELY

These words mean exact(ly), precise(ly). More perhaps than any other adjective and adverb they are today used unthinkingly and unnecessarily, both in speech and in writing, with a vague idea of adding emphasis to something that needs no emphasising. Some years ago it was fashionable among young people to give an affirmative answer by saying " definitely " and a negative one by saying " definitely not ". Always mistrust these words, and never use them unless you are sure that you would not express your meaning properly without them. A typical example of the superfluous *definite* is:

> This has caused two definite spring breakages to loaded vehicles.

See also SPECIFIC.

DEFINITIVE

This is a word borrowed from the French, meaning " final ". It differs from *definite* by importing the idea of finality. A definite offer is an offer precise in its terms. A definitive offer is an offer which the person making it declares to be his last word.

DEPEND

It is wrong to omit the *on* or *upon* after depend, as in:

> It depends whether we have received another consignment by then.

DEPENDANT and DEPENDENT

In the ordinary usage of today *dependant* is a noun meaning " a person who depends on another for support, position, etc. " (O.E.D.). *Dependent* is an adjective meaning relying on or subject to something else. Dependants are dependent on the person whose dependants they are.

DEPRECATE and DEPRECIATE

To *deprecate* is to plead against or to express disapproval of ; to *depreciate* is to lower the value of, or to belittle.

DESIDERATE and DESIDERATUM

Desiderate is a rather pedantic word. It is not, as some think, a formal synonym of *desire*, or *ask for*. It means to *feel the want of*, to *miss*, to *think long for*, as the Irish say. Thus *desideratum* means something you feel the lack of.

DESIRE

This is one of the many words that minister to a misguided striving after dignity. It is a good and useful word in its proper place, but in ordinary correspondence a humbler word is often better.

I am desirous of settling the account. (I should like to settle.)

It is thought that you will be desirous of . . . (I expect you will want . . .)

The Department is unable to issue a permit as desired. (The Department is unable to issue the permit you ask for.)

DEVELOP

This word is overworked, especially in official writings. It is only appropriate to convey the idea of a gradual unfolding or building up. Do not use it as a synonym for *arise*, *occur*, *happen*, *take place*, *come*.

Typical examples of its misuse are " shortages of raw materials may develop " (for " raw materials may become scarce ") and " rising prices might develop " (for " prices might rise ").

DIFFER

In the sense of to be different, the idiom is to differ *from*.

In the sense of to disagree, it is either to differ *from* or to differ *with*, which you please.

DIFFERENT

There is good authority for *different to*, but *different from* is today the established usage. Careless writers sometimes slip into *different than* (e.g. " it turned out differently than what I thought it would "), but for this there is no authority at all.

DILEMMA

This is a word of precise meaning, and should not be abused. It ought not to be treated as the equivalent of a difficulty, or, colloquially, of a fix or a jam. To be in a dilemma (or, if you want to show your learning, to be on the horns of a dilemma) is to be faced with two (and only two) alternative courses of action, each of which is likely to have awkward results.

DIRECT and DIRECTLY

Direct, although an adjective, is also no less an adverb than *directly*. To avoid ambiguity, it is well to confine *directly* to its meaning of *immediately* in time, and so avoid the possibility of confusion between " he is going to Edinburgh direct " and " he is going to Edinburgh directly ". Here are two examples from recent departmental circulars, the first of the right use of *direct* and the second of the wrong use of *directly*:

Committees should notify departments direct of the names and addresses of the banks.

He will arrange directly with the authority concerned for the recruitment and training of technicians.

DIS *see* De and Dis

DISASSOCIATE

Disassociate shows signs of supplanting *dissociate.* This should be discouraged; there is nothing that *disassociate* can do that *dissociate* cannot, and *dissociate* is shorter.

DISINTERESTED

Disinterested means " unbiased by personal interest " (O.E.D.). It is sometimes used wrongly for *uninterested* (i.e. not interested). A Minister recently said in the course of a speech in Parliament:

> I hope that [what I have said] will excuse me from the charge of being disinterested in this matter.

A public man dealing with public business can never be " charged " with being disinterested, as if it were a crime. It is his elementary duty always to be so.

DISPOSAL and DISPOSITION

For some purposes these words are interchangeable ; for others they are so different that there is no danger of confusion. " When doubt arises ", says Fowler, " it is worth while to remember that *disposition* corresponds to *dispose*, and *disposal* to *dispose of* ". Thus *disposition* is the word for orderly arrangement and *disposal* the word for getting rid of.

DISTANT

" In the not-distant future " and " in the not-too-distant future " are favourite phrases today. They can have no advantage over plainer ones such as " fairly soon " and " before long ", and they have the disadvantage of being tainted by a flavour of facetious understatement.

DONATE

This word is not commonly current in this country ; it offends many people ; it is unnecessary (for *give* will always do as well), and it should be avoided. Sir Alan Herbert says of it:

> The plain truth about the verb *donate* is that it is a snob-word ; for Lady Lavender *donates* her £5 to the Fund, but Mrs. Pewter's half-a-crown is only *given.*

DOUBLE NEGATIVE *see* Negative

DOUBLE PASSIVES

Grammarians condemn such constructions as the following: indeed they condemn themselves by their contorted ugliness:

> The report that is proposed to be made.
> Several amendments were endeavoured to be inserted.

A question was threatened to be put on the paper.

A sensational atmosphere is attempted to be created.

Seventy-five people are feared to have been killed in a collision.

Anyone who finds that he has written a sentence like this should recast it, e.g. " the proposed report ", " attempts were made to insert several amendments ", " a threat was made to put a question on the paper ", " an attempt is being made to create a sensational atmosphere ", " it is feared that 75 people have been killed ".

DOUBT

Idiom requires *whether* after a positive statement and *that* after a negative.

I doubt whether he will come today.

I have no doubt that he will come today.

DUE TO

Owing to long ago established itself as a prepositional phrase. But *due to* should be treated as an adjective and have a noun to agree with.

Due to is rightly used in:

The closing of the telephone exchange was due to lack of equipment. (*Due to* agrees with closing.)

The delay in replying has been due to the fact that it was hoped to call upon you. (*Due to* agrees with delay.)

Due to is wrongly used in:

We must apologise to listeners who missed the introduction to the talk due to a technical fault.

It is not possible for me to complete the work due to the fact that the premises seem not to be ready.

(*Due to the fact that* is a clumsy way of saying *because*. *See* FACT THAT.)

The scientists who have been stranded on Stonington Island due to the ice formation. . . .

It cannot however be denied that the prepositional use of *due to* is very common, especially in the United States, and may establish itself here. In 1926 Fowler said of it:

Perhaps idiom will beat the illiterates; perhaps the illiterates will beat idiom; our grandsons will know.

And an American writer, Professor Kenyon, said in 1930:

Strong as is my own prejudice against the prepositional use of *due to*, I greatly fear it has staked its claim and squatted in our midst alongside of and in exact imitation of *owing to*, its aristocratic neighbour and respected fellow-citizen.*

---

* Quoted in Perrin, *Writer's Guide and Index to English.*

EACH

(i) When *each* is the subject of a sentence the verb is singular and so is any pronoun:

Each has a room to himself.

When a plural noun or pronoun is the subject, with *each* in apposition, the verb is plural:

They have a room each.

(ii) There is a belief that *each other* is the right expression when only two persons or things are referred to, and *one another* when there are more than two. But Fowler, quoted with approval by Jespersen, says of this so-called rule " This differentiation is neither of present utility nor based on historical usage ".

For *between each*, *see* Between.

See also They for He or She.

E.G. and I.E.

These are sometimes confused, especially by the wrong use of i.e. to introduce an example. I.e. (id est) means " that is " and introduces a definition, as one might say " we are meeting on the second Tuesday of this month, i.e. the tenth ". E.g. (exempli gratia) means " for the sake of example " and introduces an illustration, as one might say " let us meet on a fixed day every month, e.g. the second Tuesday ".

EFFECT *see* Affect

EITHER

Either means one or other of two. Its use in the sense of each of two, as in:

On either side the river lie
Long fields of barley and of rye,

or in:

The concert will be broadcast on either side of the nine o'clock news,

is common, but, according to Fowler " is archaic and should be avoided except in verse or special contexts."

Either must take a singular verb. It is often wrongly given a plural one by attraction.

I am unable to trace that either of the items have been paid. (*Have* should be *has.*)

END (TO THIS END)

" To this end " shows signs of becoming a cliché (*see* CLICHÉ) in official writing. Other similar phrases such as " with this object " and " for this purpose " should not be neglected.

ENQUIRY and INQUIRY

These have long existed together as alternative spellings of the same word. In America *inquiry* is dislodging *enquiry* for all purposes. In England a useful distinction is developing : *enquiry* is used for asking a question and *inquiry* for making an investigation. Thus you might enquire what time the inquiry begins.

ENTAIL

This word is too popular. It is freely used where some other word such as *need*, *cause*, *impose*, *necessitate*, *involve*, might be more appropriate, or at least make a refreshing change. Sometimes *entail* intrudes where no verb is needed, a common habit of *involve*. *See* INVOLVE.

> . . . a statement in writing that you are willing to bear the cost entailed of opening the case, withdrawing this amount and resealing.

If *entailed* is used, the preposition should be *in*.

ENVISAGE

There is a place for *envisage* to indicate a mental vision of something planned but not yet created, but not nearly such a big place as is given to it. Do not use it where another word is more accurate.

> Mr. X said that he envisaged that there would be no access to the school from the main road (thought).

> I would refer to your letter of the 26th February, 1948, in which you envisaged the repairs would be completed by the end of this month (said that you expected).

> Certain items will fall to be dealt with not by transfer to the Minister but in the way envisaged in Section 60 (described).

EQUALLY

Do not let *as* intrude between *equally* and the word it qualifies. Not *equally as good*, but *equally good*.

ESSENTIAL

During the war our lives were regulated at every turn by the distinction between what was and what was not " essential " for what we used to call the " war-effort ". Thus the word *essential* became very familiar to us, and it remains familiar now that much the same is true of the " economic effort ". But we must not allow familiarity to lead us into absurdity. To write " I can only deal with applications of a highly essential nature " may perhaps just be allowed to pass; though it is always better to say what you mean, and in this case what you mean is: " I can only deal with applications from people doing ' highly essential ' work ". But we must draw the line at :

> It is confirmed that as a farmer you are granted high essentiality.

This means, I think, " as a farmer you are high on our waiting list ", and that would be a more intelligible thing to say. It is so easy to forget that what has a perfectly plain meaning for the writer may be gibberish to the reader.

> It is impossible to approve importation from the U.S.A. unless there is a compelling case of essentiality.

This really means, presumably, " unless it is of something that we vitally need ".

EVACUATE

Fifty years ago a writer would have been taken to task for using this word in the sense of *remove*. A place could properly be said to be evacuated, but not the people in it. This is no longer so, but the word is too much used by official writers, and everyone who finds himself using it should pause and consider whether some more commonplace word (such as remove) would not serve his purpose better.

Why, for instance, should we be told that British residents in a disturbed foreign country have been advised to evacuate their children ? When the simple verb *send away* is available, why choose one which reference to the dictionary shows to have the following primary meanings ? :

To clear out the contents of
To relinquish the occupation of (of an army)
To make void
To get rid of a disease or humour
To void, discharge
To pump out, leaving a vacuum

EVEN

This adverb, like *only* (*see* ONLY) has a way of getting into the wrong place. The importance of putting it in the right place is aptly illustrated in the *A.B.C. of English Usage* thus:

> Sentence : " I am not disturbed by your threats ".

(i) Even I am not disturbed by your threats (let alone anybody else).
(ii) I am not even disturbed by your threats (let alone hurt, annoyed, injured, alarmed).
(iii) I am not disturbed even by your threats (*even* modifies the phrase, the emphasis being on the threats).

It is also possible, though perhaps rather awkward, to put *even* immediately before *your*, and so give *your* the emphasis (your threats, let alone anybody else's).

EVENT and EVENTUALITY

Do not say *in the event of* when you might say *if*, or *in that eventuality* when you might say *if so.*

EVENTUATE

This word, says Fowler, is chiefly used in flabby journalese. It is not unknown in official writing. There are plenty of simpler words with similar meaning to choose from—*happen*, *occur*, *result*, *come about*, *turn out.*

See MATERIALISE, which is also overworked in much the same way.

EVINCE

This rather grand word should not be used in preference to simpler ones like *show*, *manifest*, *display*, *indicate*, *reveal.*

EXPERIENCE

Experience as a verb is the stilted converse of the stilted *occasion. See* OCCASION. The difficulty or inconvenience that X occasions Y experiences.

The Department is at present experiencing an acute shortage of labour.

The difficulties you are experiencing are appreciated by me.

I regret that you are experiencing difficulty with your apparatus.

Experience is well-established as a verb, but it is a stiff one and is used too much in such sentences as those just quoted from official letters. There is no great harm in it in the first example, but the other two are capable of improvement. For instance:

I recognise your difficulties. (Note also the clumsiness of the third person passive.)

I am sorry you are having difficulty with your apparatus.

EXPLANATION

Explanation must be in simple language if it is to serve its purpose. Above all it must get away from legal language, which is almost always difficult to understand.

> With reference to your letter of the 12th August, I have to state in answer to question 1 thereof that where particulars of a partnership are disclosed to the Executive Council the remuneration of the individual partner for superannuation purposes will be deemed to be such proportion of the total remuneration of such practitioners as the proportion of his share in the partnership profits bears to the total proportion of the shares of such practitioner in those profits.

This is a good example of how not to explain. I think it means merely " Your income will be taken to be the same proportion of the firm's remuneration as you used to get of its profits ". I may be wrong, but even so I cannot believe that language is unequal to any clearer explanation than the unfortunate correspondent received.

Even if the explanation had been a clear one the letter would have been damned by the pomposity of " I have to state in answer to question 1 thereof ".

Here is another explanation that is faulty for the same reason, that it does not shake off the shackles of legal language:

> Separate departments in the same premises are treated as separate premises for this purpose where separate branches of work which are commonly carried on as separate businesses in separate premises are carried on in separate departments in the same premises.

This is an example of that mathematical arrangement of words that lawyers adopt in order to make their meaning unambiguous. Worked out as one would work out an equation, the sentence serves its purpose ; as literature, it is balderdash. The explanation could easily have been given in some such way as this:

> If branches of work commonly carried on as separate businesses are carried on in separate departments of the same premises, those departments will be treated as separate premises.

It is worth remembering how often an unruly sentence like this can be reduced to order by turning part of it into an " if " clause.

Here is an example from America of an explanation which leaves the thing explained more obscure than it was before.

The New Yorker of the 17th August, 1948, quotes from a publication called " Systems Magazine ":

> Let us paraphrase and define work simplification as " that method of accomplishing a necessary purpose omitting nothing necessary to

that purpose in the simplest fashion is best ". This definition is important for it takes the mystery out of work simplification and leaves the essentials clearly outlined and succinctly stated.

The New Yorker's comment is: " It does indeed ".

The feeling that prompts you to tell your correspondent everything when explaining is commendable, but you will often help him more by resisting it, and confining yourself to the facts that are necessary in order that he may understand what has happened.

> I regret however that the Survey Officer who is responsible for the preliminary investigation as to the technical possibility of installing a telephone at the address quoted by any applicant has reported that owing to a shortage of a spare pair of wires to the underground cable (a pair of wires leading from the point near your house right back to the local exchange and thus a pair of wires essential for the provision of telephone service for you) is lacking and that therefore it is a technical impossibility to install a telephone for you at . . .

This explanation is obscure partly because the sentence is too long (*see* SENTENCES), partly because the long parenthesis has thrown the grammar out of gear (*see* PARENTHESIS), and partly because the writer, with the best intentions, says far more than is necessary even for a thoroughly polite and convincing explanation. It might have run thus:

> I am sorry to have to tell you that we have found that there is no spare pair of wires on the cable that would have to be used to connect your house with the exchange. I fear therefore that it is technically impossible to install a telephone for you.

In the following letter from a county Territorial Association that I have called the " Xshire " to another that I have called the " Yshire ", the writer has let his anxiety to tell the whole truth run right away with him:

> With reference to your memo. T/O/8 Pending dated 16/10/45 above man is not serving now in 4th Xshire Bn. H.G., having been posted from that unit to the 2nd Xshire Bn. H.G. and then reposted from the 2nd Xshire Bn. H.G. to 8th Yshire Bn. H.G. (see reverse side of AFW3066 in your possession). As we have previously explained to you under our memo. . . . the reason why we applied to you under our reference . . . dated . . . for AFW3066 showing his personal service, was because we were under the impression that he had been discharged from the 8th Yshire Bn. H.G., as prior to the above information having been traced, when this man was posted from the 2nd Xshire Bn. H.G. to the 8th Yshire Bn. H.G. instead of original AFW3066 being forwarded to you, his re-enrolment form in the 2nd Xshire Bn. H.G., was sent. Later this man's name was connected up with the original AFW3066 in our " untraceable " files of the 4th Xshire Bn. H.G., and we then incorrectly came to the conclusion—not having both AFWs3066 in our possession to compare dates of enrolment—that this man was discharged from the 8th Yshire Bn. H.G. and the AFW3066 already sent to you

upon this member's posting from the 2nd Xshire Bn. H.G. to 8th Yshire Bn. H.G. was his original AFW3066 instead of re-enrolment, and therefore applied to you for same as "Previous Service". However this matter has now been put in order at our end, the Xshire Battalions in question having amended their Part II Orders accordingly. The AFW3066 which you are now holding is the original, and we have cancelled the re-enrolment in our possession.

It is regretted that this is so involved, but we hope we have now made the matter clear to you.

FACT THAT

The fact that is an expression sometimes necessary and proper, but sometimes a clumsy way of saying what might be said more simply. When it is preceded by *in view of* or *owing to* or *in spite of* it may be merely an intricate way of saying *because* or *although*.

Owing to the fact that the exchange is working to full capacity. (Because the exchange . . .)

I was not aware of the fact that the report had been published. (I did not know that the report had been published.)

The delay in replying has been due to the fact that it was hoped to arrange for a representative to call upon you. (I delayed replying because I hoped to arrange for a representative to call on you.)

Here again observe how much easier it is to write naturally if you use the first and second persons rather than the third.

FACTITIOUS and FICTITIOUS

Factitious means "engineered" in the derogatory sense of that word, i.e. not naturally or spontaneously created. Fictitious means sham, counterfeit, unreal. A factitious thing may be genuine ; a fictitious thing cannot.

FAR (SO FAR AS . . . CONCERNED) *see* CONCERNED

FAVOUR

Do not use *favour* in the sense that has been discredited by being overdone in commercialese:

Re your esteemed favour of the 24th ult.

Your account is enclosed for favour of your kind attention.

The insertion of *favour* is no doubt prompted by politeness, and to that extent is praiseworthy. But it is a perfunctory sort of politeness at best, and "for favour of your kind attention" is all padding anyway. There is no reason to explain why an account of money owing is enclosed. We all know only too well.

See COMMERCIALESE.

FEASIBLE

Good writers do not use this word in any other sense than that of *practicable, capable of being done*. It should not be used as a synonym for *probable* or *plausible*.

FEATURE

Feature should not be used as a verb in serious writing. It may reach that status some day, but it has not done so yet. Leave it to the film industry for the present.

FEWER *see* LESS

FICTITIOUS *see* FACTITIOUS

FIRST and FIRSTLY

There used to be a grammarians' rule that you must not write *firstly*; your enumeration must be: *first, secondly, thirdly*. It was one of those arbitrary rules whose observance was supposed by a certain class of purist to be a hall-mark of correct writing. This rule, unlike many of the sort, had not even logic on its side. Of late years there has been a rebellion against these rules, and I do not think that any contemporary grammarian will mind much whether you say *first* or *firstly*.

FIRST TWO

For upward of a hundred years pretty arguments have been carried on from time to time round the question whether one should say *the first two* or *the two first*. Some famous grammarians, notably Dean Alford and Jespersen, have supported *the two first*, but the majority of expert opinion is overwhelmingly against them. So *the first two* holds the field. But the point is not important. Everyone knows what you mean, whichever you say.

FOLLOWING

Grammarians do not admit *following* as a preposition, though its use as one is becoming so common that they may soon have to give it *de facto* recognition. The orthodox view is that it is the participle of the verb *follow*, and must have a noun to agree with. Used as a preposition, it usurps the place of *after* or *in consequence of*, or *in accordance with*.

> Following our talk I am puzzled as to the reason for your letter . . . I am investigating the position and I will write to you further following the completion of my enquiries.

Here *after* will do in both places.

> It has been brought to my notice following a recent visit of an Inspector of this Ministry to the premises of . . . that you are an insured person under the Act.

Two Malays have been arrested following the attack yesterday on the Governor of Sarawak.

Here it stands for *in consequence of* or *as a result of.*

Following talks between the Railway Executive and the Union, it is proposed to reintroduce lodging terms in the Eastern Region.

After or *as a result of* is proper here.

It has a foolish air where it looks as if it were a participle agreeing with a noun or pronoun but makes nonsense if so read.

Following the orchestral concert, we come to a talk by Mr. X.

But its use is grammatical where it really does agree with a noun or pronoun.

Such rapid promotion, following his exceptional services, was not unexpected.

FOLLOWS (AS FOLLOWS)

Do not write *as follow* for *as follows*, however numerous may be the things that follow. " The construction in *as follows* is impersonal, and the verb should always be used in the singular " (O.E.D.).

FORECAST

The past tense (like the past tense of *cast*) is *forecast*, not *forecasted.*

FOREGO and FORGO

To *forego* is to go before (the foregoing provisions of this Act). To *forgo* is to go without, to waive (he will forgo his right).

FORMER and LATTER

Use *former* and *latter* sparingly, and only when they follow so closely the words to which they refer that the reader does not have to look back to see which is which.

Remember that *former* and *latter* can refer to only two things and if you use them of more than two you may puzzle your reader. If you want to refer otherwise than specifically to the last of more than two things, say *last* or *last-mentioned*, not *latter.*

FRACTION *see* PERCENTAGE

FULL STOP

Full-stops should be plentiful. To say this is to say that sentences should be short; and that is one of the first requisites in making your meaning readily understandable. *See* SENTENCES.

Always choose the full-stop rather than some slighter stop when what follows has no real connexion with what goes before. The following is the final sentence of a Press announcement of the beginning of a new term at a public school:

> There are about 630 boys in the school, and the term will end on April 1.

It can hardly be supposed that the fixing of breaking-up day depended in any way on the number of boys in the school. There should have been a full-stop after school, and " the term will end on April 1 " should have been a separate sentence.

FUNCTION

The verb *to function* has established itself, and is recognised by the dictionaries. But it is something of a newcomer, and there are still those who do not like it. For this reason some other word—*work*, for instance, or *operate*, or *perform*—should be preferred when it will do as well.

> *Function* as a verb, say Whitten and Whitaker, in the sense of *act* or *proceed with* is shoddy English. The sentence " The Council declined to function ", i.e. to act, is an example. Used of machinery (" the engine refused to function ") the verb is admissible.

FURTHERMORE

This is a prosy word, used too often. It may be difficult to avoid in cumulative argument (" Moreover . . . in addition . . . too . . . also . . . again . . . furthermore ") but sometimes it, like all its synonyms, may be mere padding. *See* PADDING. Even when it is not, one of the simpler words should be preferred, if they have not been used up.

FUSED PARTICIPLE *see* ING-ENDINGS

GERUND *see* ING-ENDINGS

GLOBAL

The meaning *spherical* is an archaism, and the meaning *world-wide* a novelty ; both should be avoided. The standard current meaning is " pertaining to or embracing the totality of a group of items, categories or the like ". Thus the price paid by the State for the coal industry was arrived at by taking a " global " figure as the value of the industry as a whole, and not an " aggregate " figure of the values of the separate collieries. The word is enjoying a spell of popular favour; it is made too much of, and used in many senses which it will not bear. Do not use either it, or *overall* (*see* OVERALL), as a showy substitute for *total* or *aggregate*.

GOBBLEDYGOOK

I was puzzled about the right title for this section. Its contents were at first in three different sections with the titles POMPOSITY, WOOLLINESS, and WORDINESS. But these overlapped too much to be kept apart. What would be a suitable title to embrace them all? I thought of OFFICIALESE, but that seemed to me hardly fair. It is true that these faults—stiffness, verbosity, woolliness and circumlocution—are not foreign to officialese, but they are not confined to it. I thought also of JARGON. But that has not the meaning I want, although it is often used as if it had. *See* JARGON. One of Ivor Brown's words—*Gargantuan*, *Pudder*, or *Barnacular*—would have done nicely. But this new American word is unique in its onomatopoeic quality. Many of the new words that America exports to us we at first eye primly, perhaps even with aversion; but occasionally one turns up which fills a gap so aptly that we find it irresistible and welcome it with open arms.* *Gobbledygook* seems to me to be a word of that sort: if my adoption of it does anything towards popularising it over here, I shall have done my country some service.

A large part of this book is directed against the style known in the United States as gobbledygook. This is not easy to define. It is certainly not merely a matter of using long and unusual words; there are dangers in supposing that it is. So many wise men throughout the centuries, from Aristotle to Mr. Winston Churchill, have emphasised the importance of using short and simple words, that long words may be in peril of being treated with less respect than they deserve. If the choice is between two words that convey a writer's meaning equally well, one short and familiar and the other long and unusual, of course the short and familiar should be preferred. But one that is long and unusual should not be rejected merely on that account if it is more apt in meaning. Mr. Churchill himself does not hesitate to prefer *flocculent* to *woolly* and *liquidate* to *destroy* if he thinks that the more uncommon word will be more effective in transferring what is in his mind into his readers'. Moreover there is an ugliness of shortness as well as an ugliness of length. On the same day in different daily papers I have seen the same official referred to as "Administrator of the Organisation for European Economic Cooperation" and as "Aid Boss".

---

* The newcomer *teenager* ought surely to be so treated by a country that at present has to choose between *youth*, which applies to one sex only, *young person*, which suggests a Victorian butler introducing a candidate for the post of kitchen-maid, and *juvenile*, which seems to have struck up a permanent liaison with *delinquency*.

Neither title is euphonious, and few would unhesitatingly prefer the short one.

Gobbledygook is a composite quality. The main object of this book is to analyse and classify its manifestations, and to write something about each under a heading appropriate to it. Examples are the headings ABSTRACT WORDS, ARRANGEMENT, CLICHÉ, EXPLANATION, INVOLVE, JARGON, METAPHOR, NOUN-ADJECTIVES, PADDING, PARENTHESIS, POSITION, PREPOSITIONS, SENTENCES, among many others. I have in fact attempted what, if I were writing gobbledygook, I should call a " breakdown " of gobbledygook. *See* BREAKDOWN. Under the present general heading are collected a few examples, not easily classifiable, of those elements of gobbledygook that might be labelled *pomposity*, *circumlocution*, *woolliness* and *wordiness*, and a suggested translation of each into plain words :

Example	Translation
An essential prerequisite to the adequate fulfilment of the dual functions of research and teaching is an atmosphere of freedom and progress.	Teaching and research can only be adequately carried on in an atmosphere of freedom and progress.
There is a complete lack of ablution facilities.	There is nowhere to wash.
In the initial stages.	At first.
Circumstances which obtained prior to the outbreak of hostilities.	Conditions before the war.
If they make a nil determination of need.	If they decide there is no case for giving anything.
Was this the realisation of an anticipated liability ?	Did you expect that you would have to do this ?
The position regarding this matter is that owing to the fact that two claims were made by two claimants of the same name some confusion arose.	Confusion arose because there were two claimants with the same name.

See POSITION and FACT THAT.

I should be glad if you would be good enough to confirm the settlement and it would be of assistance to me if you are prepared to state the terms thereof and the approximate proportion of the full claim which such settlement represents.	Will you please confirm the settlement. It would help me if you tell me its terms, and how the amount compares with your full claim.

Example	Translation
Having regard to these different considerations and the evidence available, the general conclusion in the light of the latest investigation is that there is no definite scientific justification either for national measures aimed at reducing appreciably the rook population or for encouraging its increase. . . . This accords with what is understood to be the Ministry's present attitude to the rook.	All this leads us to the conclusion that no case can be made out for encouraging either the killing of rooks or their protection. This, we understand, accords with the Ministry's present policy.
I would suggest therefore that this firm's production from an output point of view is determined with regard to each of these main headings, and then it would be advisable to approach Mr. X so that he may have this firm's requirements considered by the correct departments.	I suggest that this firm's output should be stated under these headings, and referred to Mr. X so that he may have their requirements considered by the right departments.

(This illustrates the tendency of phrases like " point of view " and " with regard to " to produce woolly writing. Here " production from an output point of view " means no more than " output " and " determined with regard to these headings " means " stated under these headings ".)

The Committee have decided to grant the application, subject to the exclusion of the provision of general medical services by you in those parts of the . . . area where the Committee declared the number of doctors to be adequate. . . . Such restriction is subject to the right of appeal against the decision of the Committee to the Minister.	The Committee grant you leave to practise except in those parts of the area where they have declared the number of doctors to be adequate. You have the right to appeal to the Minister against this limitation.
In this connexion I am to say that before the Department can assess the value of the plant, it will be necessary for them to receive from you, through this office, details of the items in question rendered on the appropriate forms. It would be appreciated therefore if you	Before the Department can assess the value of the plant they must have details of it on the appropriate forms. Will you therefore please complete the enclosed form and return it with five copies of the schedule.

Example	Translation
would complete the enclosed form with the required information, and return the schedule in quintuplicate to this office at the above address.	

The following example and the suggested translation of it are taken from the *Municipal Review*:

The object of sifting these waiting lists is to ascertain the existing live demand for houses required to meet the needs of families who are not satisfactorily housed and also to secure that the lists are not inflated by retention on them of those who, since their application, have removed from the district, have found accommodation for themselves, or for other reasons do not now desire to be considered.	These lists should be sifted to find out how many families still want houses and to eliminate those who no longer need or wish to be considered.

The following is from the *British Medical Journal*:

Imitation " legalese " is far more annoying to read than the genuine article, yet it abounds in letters running on administrative errands throughout the health service. A correspondent tells us that a regional hospital board sent him a letter asking him to certify that the candidate for a job " is free from any physical defect or disease which now impairs her capacity satisfactorily to undertake the duties of the post for which she is a candidate ". The writer of the letter apparently quoted this curious phrase from another document, presumably because he felt that he would be sailing across an uncharted sea if he asked our correspondent to certify that the candidate was fit for the job.

Lastly, a piece of gobbledygook that defies translation:

To reduce the risk of war and establish conditions of lasting peace requires the closer co-ordination in the employment of their joint resources to underpin these countries' economics in such a manner as to permit the full maintenance of their social and material standards as well as to adequate development of the necessary measures."

GOT

Have got, for *possess* or *have*, says Fowler, is good colloquial but not good literary English. Others have been more lenient. Dr. Johnson said:

" He has got a good estate " does not always mean that he has acquired, but barely that he possesses it. So we say " the lady has got black eyes ", merely meaning that she has them.

And Dr. Ballard has written*:

> What is wrong with the word? Its pedigree is beyond reproach. If the reader will consult the Oxford English Dictionary he will find that Shakespeare uses the word. So does Swift; Ruskin uses it frequently, and Augustine Birrell in OBITER DICTA asks "What has the general public got to do with literature?" Johnson in his Dictionary gives possession as a legitimate meaning of the verb to get, and quotes George Herbert. Indeed he uses it himself in a letter to Boswell. The only inference we can draw is that it is not a real error but a counterfeit invented by schoolmasters.

When such high authorities differ, what is the plain man to think? If it is true, as I hold it to be, that superfluous words are an evil, we ought to condemn "the lady has got black eyes", but not "the lady has got a black eye". Still, writing for those whose prose inclines more often to primness than to colloquialisms, and who are not likely to overdo the use of *got*, I advise them not to be afraid of it. This at least is certain: that it is better to say "I have got the information you wanted" than "I have obtained the information which you desired".

GROUP

This word in its statistical sense should be used with discretion. There is a coldness and inhumanity in describing people as *groups*, though it is not so bad as describing them as *brackets*. *See* BRACKETS. The writer of the sentence "these are likely in the main to be bought by the lower income groups" would have expressed his meaning more plainly if he had written "these are likely in the main to be bought by people with small incomes". *Income Group* has become a cliché. *See* CLICHÉ.

HAND (TO HAND)

Do not use the expression *to hand* in the sense of *received*. It is one of those commercial clichés that do not mean anything.

> I thank you for your letter of the 15th inst., which came to hand on the 18th idem.

It would be better to say "which was received. . . ."

As to *inst* and *idem*, *see* INST.

See also COMMERCIALESE.

---

* *Teaching and Testing English.* The same writer's *Thought and Language* contains an even longer and even more spirited defence of *got*.

HARD and HARDLY

Hard, not *hardly*, is the adverb of the adjective *hard*. *Hardly* must not be used except in the sense of *scarcely*. *Hardly earned* and *hard-earned* have quite different meanings.

Hardly, like *scarcely*, is followed by *when*, not by *than*, in such a sentence as " I had hardly begun when I was interrupted ". *Than* sometimes creeps in from a false analogy with " I had no sooner begun than I was interrupted ".

HELP

The expression " more than one can help " is a literal absurdity. It means exactly the opposite of what it says. " I won't be longer than I can help " means " I won't be longer than is unavoidable ", that is to say, longer than I *can't* help. But it is good English idiom.

> They will not respect more than they can help treaties exacted from them under duress. (Winston Churchill, *The Gathering Storm*).

Writers who find the absurdity of the phrase more than they can stomach can always write " more than they must " instead.

HERETO, HEREWITH, THERETO, THEREWITH

Avoid as far as possible full-dress compounds of this kind unless, like *therefore*, they have become part of every-day language. Most of them put a flavour of legalism into any document in which they are used. Use a preposition and pronoun instead.

> With reference to the second paragraph thereof. (With reference to its second paragraph.)
>
> I have received your letter and thank you for the information contained therein. (I thank you for the information contained in your letter.)
>
> I am to ask you to explain the circumstances in which the gift was made and to forward any correspondence relative thereto. (. . . any correspondence about it.)

Do not say " I enclose herewith ". *Herewith* adds nothing to the sense. All it does is to put a touch of starch into the letter.

HOPE

Hope should not be used in the passive except in the impersonal phrase *it is hoped*. We may say " It is hoped that payment will be made next week ", or " payment is expected to be made next week ", but not " payment is hoped to be made next week ". *See* DOUBLE PASSIVES.

HYPHEN

In *Modern English Usage* Fowler makes an elaborate study of the hyphen. He begins engagingly by pointing out that " superfluous hair-remover " can only mean a hair-remover that nobody wants, and he proceeds to work out a code of rules for the proper use of the hyphen. He admits that the result of following his rules " will often differ from current usage ". But, he adds, " that usage is so variable as to be better named caprice ". The author of the style-book of the Oxford University Press of New York (quoted in Perrin's *Writer's Guide*) strikes the same note when he says " If you take hyphens seriously you will surely go mad ".

I have no intention of taking hyphens seriously. Those who wish to do so I leave to Fowler's eleven columns. If I attempted to lay down any rules I should certainly go astray, and give advice not seemly to be followed. For instance, the general practice of hyphening *co* when it is attached as a prefix to a word beginning with a vowel has always seemed to me absurd, especially as it leads to such possibilities of misunderstanding as *unco-ordinated* must present to a Scotsman. If it is objected that ambiguity may result, and readers may be puzzled whether *coop* is something to put a hen in or a profit-sharing association, this should be removed by a diaeresis (*coöp*) not a hyphen (*co-op*). That is what a diaeresis is for.

I will attempt no more than to give a few elementary warnings.

(i) Do not use hyphens unnecessarily. Write, for instance, *today*, not *to-day*, *halfpenny* not *half-penny*, *motor car*, not *motor-car*. If you must use *overall* as an adjective (though this is not recommended) write it like that, and not *over-all*. *See* OVERALL.

(ii) If you do split a word with a hyphen, make sure you split it at the main break. Though you may write *self-conscious*, if you wish to have a hyphen in the word, you must not write *unself-conscious* but *un-selfconscious*.

(iii) To prevent ambiguity a hyphen should always be used in a compound adjective (e.g. *well-written*, *first-class*, *six-inch*, *copper-coloured*). The omission of a hyphen between *government* and *financed* in the following sentence throws the reader on to a false scent:

> When Government financed projects in the development areas have been grouped. . . .

(iv) Do not be guilty of the slovenly habit of putting extraneous words inside a hyphenated pair of words. Not even scarcity of paper can excuse writing:

Where chaplains (whole- or part-time) have been appointed.

instead of " where chaplains have been appointed, whole-time or part-time ".

I and ME

About the age-long conflict between *it is I* and *it is me*, no more need be said than that, in the present stage of the battle, most people would think " it is I " pedantic in talk and " it is me " improper in writing.

What calls more for examination is the practice of using *I* for *me* in combination with some noun or other pronoun, e.g. " between you and I ", " let you and I go ". Why this has become so prevalent is not easy to say. Perhaps it comes partly from an excess of zeal in correcting the opposite error. When Mrs. Elton said " Neither Mr. Suckling nor me had ever any patience with them ", and Lydia Bennet " Mrs. Forster and me are such friends ", they were guilty of a vulgarism that was, no doubt, common in Jane Austen's day, and is not unknown today. One might suppose that this mistake was corrected by teachers of English in our schools with such ferocity that their pupils are left with the conviction that such combinations as *you and me* are in all circumstances ungrammatical. But that will not quite do. It might explain a popular broadcaster's saying " that's four to Margaret and I ", but it cannot explain why Shakespeare wrote: " All debts are cleared between you and I ".*

It is the combination of oneself with someone else that proves fatal. The official who wrote: " I trust that it will be convenient to you for my colleague and I to call upon you next Tuesday " would never, if he had been proposing to come alone, have written " I trust that it will be convenient to you for I to call upon you. . . ." A sure and easy way of avoiding this blunder is to ask oneself what case the personal pronoun would have been in—would it have been *I* or *me*—if it had stood alone. It should remain the same in partnership as it would have been by itself.

IDEM *see* INST.

IDIOM

Idiom is defined by the O.E.D. as "a peculiarity of phraseology approved by usage and often having a meaning other than its logical or grammatical one ". When anything in this book is called " good English idiom " or " idiomatic ", what is meant

* Shakespeare is notoriously the grammarians' despair. Even Hamlet, a young man of scholarship standard if ever there was one, said " between who ? " when Polonius asked him, " What is the matter, my Lord ? "

is that usage has established it as correct. Idiom does not conflict with grammar or logic as a matter of course ; it is usually grammatically and logically neutral. Idiom requires us to say *aim at getting*, not *aim to get*, and *try to get*, not *try at getting*. Logic and grammar do not object to this, but they would be equally content with *aim to get* and *try at getting*. At the same time idiom is, in Jespersen's phrase, " a tyrannical, capricious, utterly incalculable thing ", and if logic and grammar get in its way, so much the worse for logic and grammar. It is idiomatic—at least in speech—to say " I won't be longer than I can help " and " it's me ". That the first is logically nonsense and the second a grammatical howler is neither here nor there; idiom makes light of such things.

Do not therefore listen too readily to those who say that something " must " be wrong because it is illogical or ungrammatical. If it has not established itself as idiom, then by all means let logic and grammar have their way, or there will be anarchy in the language. But grammar has no chance, and ought to have no chance, against genuine idiom. Logan Pearsall Smith says:

> Plainly a language which was all idiom and unreason would be impossible as an instrument of thought; but all languages permit the existence of a certain number of illogical expressions: and the fact that, in spite of their vulgar origin and illiterate appearance, they have succeeded in elbowing their way into our prose and poetry, and even learned lexicons and grammars, is proof that they perform a necessary function in the domestic economy of speech*.

I.E. *see* E. G.

IF

(i) *If* for *though*. *If* should not be used in the sense of *though* ; it causes ambiguity.

> The letters that come from that department are well-reasoned if long-winded.

Does *if* here mean *if* or *though* ? In the one case the sentence will mean that the long-windedness of the letters makes them well-reasoned; in the other case it will mean that they are well-reasoned in spite of their long-windedness. There is no excuse for writing an ambiguous sentence when it might have been written as easily without ambiguity. Those who get into the habit of using *if* for *though* may land themselves in such absurdities as the example given by Sir Alan Herbert:

> Milk is nourishing, if tuberculous.

---

* *Words and Idioms*. Constable & Co.

(ii) *If* for *whether*.

The use of *if* for *whether* is also a fruitful cause of ambiguity.

A form I have to fill up in order to get something I want contains the entry:

State here if cultivation contract work is undertaken.

Does this mean " state here whether cultivation contract work is undertaken, yes or no ", or does it mean " if cultivation contract work is undertaken, this is the place to say so, but if it is not you need say nothing about the subject either here or anywhere else " ? Unnecessary ambiguity should always be avoided, and ambiguity caused by using *if* instead of *whether* is wantonly unnecessary.

IF and WHEN

Do not use this expression unless you are sure that both conjunctions are needed. You rarely will be.

It is planned to take the opportunity if and when it arises.

Clearly there is no justification for both words in that sentence.

Further cases will be studied if and when the material is available.

Perhaps that is one of the rare cases in which the use of the two could be justified on this ground: that *if* alone will not do because the writer wants to emphasise that material becoming available will be studied immediately, and *when* alone will not do because it is uncertain whether the material ever will be available. But it is all rather subtle.

IMPLEMENT

This verb, meaning to carry out or fulfil, used to be hardly known outside the " barbarous jargon of the Scottish Bar"*. As recently as 1926 Fowler " could not acquit of the charge of pedantry " a writer who used the expression " implementing Labour's promises to the electorate ". It is now too firmly established to be driven out, but the occasional use of *carry out* or *fulfil* for a change would be refreshing.

IMPLY and INFER

It is a common error to use *infer* for *imply*. A writer or speaker implies what his reader or listener infers. The difference is illustrated thus by Sir Alan Herbert :

If you see a man staggering along the road you may infer that he is drunk, without saying a word; but if you say " Had one too many ? " you do not infer but imply that he is drunk.

INASMUCH AS

This is sometimes used in the sense of *so far as* and sometimes

*David Irving, quoted by Fowler.

as a clumsy way of saying *since*. It is therefore ambiguous, and might well be dispensed with altogether.

INCIDENTALLY

Incidentally, like *actually* and *definitely*, is today much used in talk, with little meaning, if any. It is just a precautionary noise. That may partly account for the use of *incidentally* in writing as an apology for irrelevance. It should not be allowed to make writers forget their duty to sustain an orderly sequence of thought.

INCLINED TO THINK

A civil service correspondent takes me to task for having dealt too leniently with this phrase in *Plain Words*. What I said was:

> Being inclined to think, in the sense of inclining to an opinion not yet crystallised, is a reasonable enough expression, just as one may say colloquially " my mind is moving that way ". But excessive use of the phrase may provoke the captious critic to say that if being inclined to think is really something different from thinking, then the less said about it the better until it has ripened into something that can be properly called thought.

My correspondent calls the phrase " a monstrosity " which he says, " the cynic regards as being typical of the civil servant, who is (in his eyes) incapable of decisive thought ". Perhaps it is wise to avoid a phrase that can arouse feelings of that sort in anyone.

INCULCATE

One *inculcates* ideas into people, not people with ideas ; *imbue* would be the right word for that. A vague association with *inoculate* may have something to do with the wrong use of *inculcate*.

INDIVIDUAL

This word should not be used as a noun except for the purpose of distinguishing between an individual and a group, as it is used in Income Tax Law to mark the distinction between a personal taxpayer and a corporate one. It should not be treated as a synonym for *person*, though this meaning (called by the O.E.D. " vulgar or disparaging ") was common in the nineteenth century, especially in Dickens, who was fond of using it facetiously. Like the French *individu*, it has acquired a contemptuous tinge. Readers of Surtees will remember that Mr. Martin Moonface's reference to Mr. Jorrocks as an " unfortunate individual " provoked the indignant retort " You are another indiwidual ".

INFER *see* IMPLY

INFORM

The less formal word *tell* is sometimes more suitable than *inform*, especially in letters that we want to make friendly.

" Please tell me ", or " Please let me know ", is less stiff than " Kindly inform me ".

Inform cannot be used with a verb in the infinitive, and the writer of this sentence has gone wrong:

> I am informing the branch to grant this application.

He should have said *telling* or *asking*.

Moreover, *inform* seems to attract adverbs as prim as itself, sometimes almost menacing. In *kindly inform me* the politeness rings hollow ; all it does is to put a frigid and magisterial tone into your request. *Perhaps you will inform me* means, in officialese, that you have *got* to inform me, and no " perhaps " about it, and I suspect the consequences may be serious for you.

INFORMATION (FOR YOUR INFORMATION)

For your information, a phrase much used in official and business letters, is almost always padding, inserted without thought and without significance.

> For your information this machine is required for the above-mentioned power station.
>
> For your information I should perhaps explain that there is still a shortage of materials.
>
> For your information I would inform you that it will be necessary for you to approach the local Agricultural Executive Committee.

This last example, taken from a letter I received myself, shows up the futility of this curious cliché. It was not even true that I was being told this " for information " ; " for action " would have been more appropriate.

ING ENDINGS

Words ending in *ing* are mostly verbal participles or gerunds, and, as we shall see, it is not always easy to say which is which. By way of introduction it will be enough to observe that when they are of the nature of participles they may be true verbs (*I was working*) or adjectives (*a working agreement*) or in rare cases prepositions (*concerning this question*) or conjunctions (*supposing this happened*) ; if they are of the nature of gerunds they are always nouns (*I am pleased at his coming*)—or rather a hybrid between a noun and a verb, for you may use the gerund with the construction either of a noun (*after the careful reading of these papers*) or of a mixture between a verb and a noun (*after carefully reading these papers*). It is most confusing, but fortunately we are seldom called on to put a label on these words, and so I have preferred to give this section an indeterminate title.

Numerous pitfalls beset the use of ing-words. Here are some of them:

(i) Absolute construction.

This is, in itself, straightforward enough. The absolute construction, in the words of the O.E.D., is a name given to a phrase " standing out of grammatical relation or syntactical construction with other words ". In the sentence " The chairman having restored order, the committee resumed ", the phrase " the chairman having restored order " forms an absolute construction.

But there is no absolute construction in the sentence " The chairman, having restored order, called on the last speaker to continue ". Here *the chairman* is the subject of the sentence.

Because of a confusion with that type of sentence, it is a curiously common error to put a comma in the absolute construction. *See* COMMA (v).

(ii) Unattached (or unrelated) participle.

This blunder is rather like the last. A writer begins a sentence with a participle (which, since it is a sort of adjective, must be given a noun to support it) and then forgets to give it its noun, thus leaving it " unattached ".

> Arising out of a collision between a removal van and a fully loaded bus in a fog, E.C.F., removal van driver, appeared on a charge of manslaughter.

Grammatically in this sentence it was the van-driver, not the charge against him, that arose out of the collision. He probably did; but that was not what the writer meant.

> Whilst requesting you to furnish the return now outstanding you are advised that in future it would greatly facilitate. . . .

Requesting is unattached. If the structure of this rather clumsy sentence is to be retained it must run " Whilst requesting you . . . I advise you that . . . "

As has been mentioned, some ing-words have won the right to be treated as prepositions. Among them are *regarding*, *considering*, *owing to*, *concerning*, *failing* and *seeing*. When any of these is used as a preposition, there can be no question of its being misused as an unattached participle:

> Considering the attack that had been made on him, his speech was moderate in tone.

If however *considering* were used not as a preposition-participle but as an adjective-participle, it could be unattached. It is so in:

> Considering the attack on him beneath his notice, his speech was moderate in tone.

Past participles, as well as present, may become unattached:

> Formal application is now being made for the necessary way-leave consent, and as soon as received the work will proceed.

Grammatically *received* can only be attached to work ; and that is nonsense. The writer should have said " as soon as this is received ".

(iii) Unattached gerund.

A gerund can become unattached in much the same way as a participle:

> Indeed we know little of Stalin's personality at all : a few works of Bolshevik theory, arid and heavy, and speeches still more impersonal, without literary grace, repeating a few simple formulas with crushing weight—after reading these Stalin appears more a myth than a man.

Grammatically " after reading these " means after Stalin has read them, not after we have.

(iv) Gerund and infinitive.

In what seems to be a completely arbitrary way, some nouns, adjectives, and verbs like to take an infinitive, and some a gerund with a preposition.

For instance:

Dislike of doing	Reluctance to do
Capable of doing	Able to do
Demur to doing	Hesitate to do

Instances could be mutiplied indefinitely. There is no rule ; it can only be a matter of observation and consulting a dictionary when in doubt.

(v) The " fused participle ".

All authorities agree that it is idiomatic English to write " the *Bill's* getting a second reading surprised everyone ": that is to say it is correct to treat *getting* as a gerund requiring *Bill's* to be in the possessive. What they are not agreed about is whether it is also correct to treat *getting* as a participle, and write " the *Bill* getting a second reading surprised everyone ". If that is a legitimate grammatical construction, the subject of the sentence, which cannot be *Bill* by itself, or *getting* by itself, must be a fusion of the two. Hence the name " fused participle ".

With a proper name or personal pronoun there is no temptation to employ a fused participle. Nobody would prefer " He coming (or Smith coming) surprised me " to " His coming (or Smith's coming) surprised me ". That is sure ground.

For the rest, it is always possible, and generally wise, to be on the safe side by turning the sentence round, and writing neither " the Bill getting, etc." (which offends some purists) nor " the Bill's getting, etc." (which sounds odd to some ears) but " everyone was surprised that the Bill got a second reading ".

INQUIRY *see* ENQUIRY

INSTANCE

Instance beguiles writers in the same way as *case* (*see* CASE) into roundabout ways of saying simple things:

> In the majority of instances the houses are three-bedroom. (Most of the houses are three-bedroom.)
>
> Most of the factories are modern, but in a few instances the plant is obsolete. (In a few of them.)

INST., ULT., PROX., IDEM

Do not use any of these curious synonyms for the name of a month. To put the name of the month itself has the double advantage of conveying your meaning with greater speed, and of avoiding all taint of commercialese.

See COMMERCIALESE.

INVERTED COMMAS

I have read nothing more sensible about inverted commas than this from the *A.B.C. of English Usage:*

> It is remarkable in an age peculiarly contemptuous of punctuation marks that we have not yet had the courage to abolish inverted commas. . . . After all, they are a modern invention. The Bible is plain enough without them ; and so is the literature of the eighteenth century. Bernard Shaw scorns them. However, since they are with us, we must do our best with them, trying always to reduce them to a minimum.

I have only two other things to say on this vexatious topic.

One is to give a warning against over-indulgence in the trick of encasing words or phrases in inverted commas to indicate that they are being used in a slang or technical or facetious or some other unusual sense. This is a useful occasional device ; instances may be found in this book. But it is a dangerous habit. It may develop into a craving for inverted commas, leading to the use of them in the same promiscuous way as Victorian letter-writers used underlinings. " I know this is not quite the right word ", the inverted commas seem to say, " but I can't be bothered to think of a better " ; or, " please note that I am using this word facetiously "; or, " don't think I don't know that this is a cliché ". If the word is the right one, do not be ashamed of it: if it is the wrong one, do not use it. It is unnecessary, for instance, to put *catchment* in inverted commas when writing of the catchment area of a hospital; the metaphor is a useful and obvious one.

The second question is whether punctuation marks (including notes of interrogation and exclamation) should come before or after the inverted commas that close a quotation. This has been much argued, with no conclusive result. It does not seem to me of great practical importance, but I feel bound to refer to it, if only because a correspondent criticised me for giving no guidance in *Plain Words* and accused me of being manifestly shaky about it myself. The truth is that there is no settled practice governing this most complicated subject. Pages were written about it by the Fowlers in *The King's English*, but their conclusions are by no means universally accepted.

There are two schools of thought. Most books on English advise that stops should be put in their logical positions. If the stops are part of the sentence quoted, put them within the inverted commas. If they are part of a longer sentence within which the quotation stands, put them outside the inverted commas. If the quotation and the sentence embracing it end together, so that each needs a stop at the same time, do not carry logic to the lengths of putting one inside and one out, but be content with the one outside. To give three simple examples of the application of this advice to question-marks :

> I said to him " Why worry ? "
> Why did you say to him " Don't worry " ?
> Why did you say to him " Why worry " ? (Strictly " Why worry ? " ?)

But most publishers will not have this. They dislike the look of stops outside inverted commas if they can possibly be put inside. Here is a typical extract from a publisher's House Rules:

> Commas, full-stops, etc., closing matter in quotation marks may be placed before the final quotation marks, whether they form part of the original extract or not, provided that no ambiguity is likely to arise as to exactly what is quoted and what is not; this rule may not be as logical as that which insists on placing the punctuation marks strictly *according to the sense*, but the printed result looks more pleasing and justifies the convention.

But we need not concern ourselves here with questions of taste in printing. The drafter of official letters and memoranda is advised to stick to the principle of placing the punctuation marks according to the sense.

INVOLVE

The meaning of this popular word has been diluted to a point of extreme insipidity. Originally it meant *wrap up in something, enfold.* Then it acquired the figurative meaning *entangle a person in difficulties or embarrassment,* and especially *implicate in crime, or a charge.* Then it began to lose colour, and to be used as though it meant nothing more than *include, contain* or *imply.* It has thus developed a vagueness that makes it the delight of those who dislike the effort of searching for the right word. It is consequently much used, generally where some more specific word would be better, and sometimes where it is merely superfluous.

This is no new phenomenon. More than forty years ago Sir Clifford Allbut, writing about the English style of medical students at Cambridge, said:

> *To involve,* with its ugly and upstart noun *involvement* has to do duty for to *attack,* to *invade,* to *injure,* to *affect,* to *pervert,* to *encroach upon,* to *influence,* to *enclose,* to *implicate,* to *permeate,* to *pervade,* to *penetrate.* to *dislocate,* to *contaminate,* and so forth.

Here are a few recent examples from official writing:

> The additional rent involved will be £1. (Omit *involved.*)
>
> There are certain amounts of the material available without permit, but the quantities involved are getting less. (Omit *involved.*)
>
> It has been agreed that the capital cost involved in the installation of the works shall be included. (. . . that the capital cost of installing . . .)
>
> An offence involving the death penalty. (An offence punishable by death.)
>
> It is some comfort to learn that the eight to thirteen bracket is the only one that involved more arrests. (. . . is the only one in which there were more arrests.) *For this use of bracket see* BRACKET.
>
> Patients desiring to pay for the extra amenity involved. (Omit *involved.*)
>
> Much labour has been involved in advertising. (Much labour has been expended on advertising.)
>
> If she is to take any part in the care of children, employment would be involved which should be put on a paid footing. (If she is to take any part in the care of children, that would be employment which . . .)

The following four examples all occur in one paragraph of a memorandum, covering less than half a page, and strikingly illustrate the ascendancy of this word over undiscriminating writers:

The Ministry have indicated that they would not favour any proposal which would involve an increase in establishment at the present time. (*Involve* here is harmless, but in order to practise shaking off its yoke, let us substitute *mean* or *lead to*.)

The Company would oppose this application unless compensation involving a substantial sum were paid. (This one cannot get off so lightly. The writer should have said " unless a substantial sum were paid in compensation ".)

We have been informed that the procedure involved would necessitate lengthy negotiation. . . . (Here *involved* is doing no work at all and should be omitted.)

This would possibly involve the creation of a precedent that might embarrass the Government. (This illustrates the greatest of the sins into which *involve* seduces the writer—that of saying *involve the creation of* instead of the simple, direct and adequate *create.*)

Such are some of the sadly flabby uses to which this word of character is put. Reserve it for more virile purposes and especially for use where there is a suggestion of entanglement or complication, as we use *involved* when we say " this is a most involved subject ". Here are two examples of its reasonable use :

This experience has thrown into high relief the complications and delays involved in the existing machinery for obtaining approval.

Mr. Menzies protested against the Australian Government's acceptance of the invitation to the conference at Delhi on the Indonesian dispute, holding that Australia ought not to be involved.

ISE or IZE

On the question whether verbs like *organise* and nouns like *organisation* should be spelt with an *s* or a *z* the authorities differ. The O.E.D. favours universal *ize*, arguing that the suffix is always in its origin either Greek or Latin and in both languages it is spelt with a *z*. Other authorities, including most English printers, recommend universal *ise*. Fowler stands between these two opinions. He points out that the O.E.D.'s advice over-simplifies the problem, since there are some verbs (e.g. *advertise*, *comprise*, *despise*, *exercise* and *surmise*) which are never spelt *ize* in this country. On the other hand, he says " the difficulty of remembering which these *ise* verbs are is the only reason for making *ise* universal, and the sacrifice of significance to ease does not seem justified ". This austere conclusion will not commend itself to everyone. It does not do so to the authors of the *A.B.C. of English Usage*, who say roundly " the advice given here is to end them all in *ise* ", a verdict with which I respectfully agree.

ITEM

This word is a great favourite, especially in business letters. It is made to mean almost anything. It is safe to say that any sentence in which this omnibus use occurs will be improved either by omitting the word or by substituting a word of more definite meaning. The following is a typical instance; it refers to the condition of a set of batteries:

> The accessory items, stands and other parts, are satisfactory, but the sediment approximates to 1-in. in depth and . . . this item can be removed conveniently when the renewals are effected.

Accessory items should be changed to *accessories* and *this item can be removed* to *this can be removed.*

The next example is from a notice of a meeting:

> * I shall be able to attend the meeting.
> * I shall not be able to attend the meeting.
> * Please delete items not required.

Here, what meant *sediment* in the first example appears to mean *words*.

JARGON

A dictionary definition of jargon is " a word applied contemptuously to the language of scholars, the terminology of a science or art, or the cant of a class, sect, trade, or profession ". When it was confined to that sense it was a useful word. But it has been handled so promiscuously of recent years that the edge has been taken off it, and now, as has been well said, it signifies little more than any speech that a person feels to be inferior to his own*.

When officials are accused of writing jargon, what is usually meant is that they affect a pompous and flabby verbosity. The Americans have a pleasant word for it—" gobbledygook ". It cannot be questioned that there is too much of that sort of thing in the general run of present-day writing, both official and other. Why this should be so, and how it can be cured, is one of the purposes of this book to examine. *See for instance* ABSTRACT WORDS, EXPLANATION, GOBBLEDYGOOK, POSITION.

But there is also a jargon in the strict sense of the word, and official writing is not free from it. Technical terms are used—especially conventional phrases invented by a government department—which are understood inside the department but are unintelligible to outsiders. That is true jargon. A circular from the headquarters of a department to its regional officers begins:

---

* Perrin, *Writer's Guide.*

The physical progressing of building cases should be confined to . . .

Nobody could say what meaning this was intended to convey unless he held the key*. It is not English, except in the sense that the words are English words. They are a group of symbols used in conventional senses known only to the parties to the convention. It may be said that no harm is done, because the instruction is not meant to be read by anyone unfamiliar with the departmental jargon. But using jargon is a dangerous habit; it is easy to forget that the public do not understand it, and to slip into the use of it in explaining things to them. If that is done, those seeking enlightenment will find themselves plunged in even deeper obscurity. *See* EXPLANATION.

Let us take another example. " Distribution of industry policy " is an expression well understood in the Board of Trade and other departments concerned with the subject. But it is jargon. Intrinsically the phrase has no certain meaning. Not even its grammatical construction is clear. So far as the words go, it is at least as likely that it refers to distributing something called " industry-policy " as to a policy of distributing industry. Even when we know that " distribution-of-industry " is a compound noun-adjective qualifying *policy*, we still do not give to the words the full meaning that those who invented the phrase intended it to have. The esoteric meaning attached to this clump of ungrammatical nonsense is the policy of exercising governmental control over the establishment of new factories in such a way as to minimise the risk of local mass unemployment. No doubt it is convenient to have a label for anything that can only be explained so cumbrously. But it must not be forgotten that what is written on the label consists of code symbols unintelligible to the outsider. If the initiated want to communicate with those who are outside their mysteries, they must use language that everyone understands.

---

* A member of the department has kindly given me this interpretation, qualified by the words " as far as I can discover ":

" 'The physical progressing of building cases' means going at intervals to the sites of factories etc. whose building is sponsored by the department and otherwise approved to see how many bricks have been laid since the last visit. 'Physical' apparently here exemplifies a portmanteau usage (? syllepsis) and refers both to the flesh-and-blood presence of the inspector and to the material development of the edifice, neither of which is, however, mentioned. 'Progressing' I gather should have the accent on the first syllable and should be distinguished from pro*gres*sing. It means recording or helping forward the progress rather than going forward. 'Cases' is the common term for units of work which consist of applying a given set of rules to a number of individual problems . . . 'should be confined to' means that only in the types of cases specified may an officer leave his desk to visit the site ".

KIND

"Those kind of things." This use of the plural *these* or *those* with the singular *kind* or *sort* is common in conversation, and instances of it could be found in good authors. But public opinion today generally condemns it. It can be avoided by writing "that kind of thing" or "things of that kind".

LACK and DEARTH

Lack is a useful word to denote a deficiency of something, and occasionally, though less commonly, the complete absence of something. But there is a lack of so many things nowadays that the word is being pressed too much into service. For instance "there is a complete lack of spare underground wire" is not the natural way of saying "we have no spare underground wire".

Dearth is misused in the same way. "A dearth of information exists" is better expressed "We know very little". This is a symptom of the abstract-word disease. *See* ABSTRACT WORDS.

LATTER *see* FORMER

LEADING QUESTION

This does not mean, as is widely supposed, a question designed to embarrass the person questioned. On the contrary, it means a question designed to help him by suggesting the answer—a type of question not permitted when a witness is being examined by the counsel who called him.

LESS and FEWER

The following is taken from *Good and Bad English* by Whitten and Whitaker:

> *Less* appertains to degree, quantity or extent; *fewer* to number. Thus, *less* outlay, *fewer* expenses; *less* help, *fewer* helpers; *less* milk, *fewer* eggs.
>
> But although *few* applies to number do not join it to the word itself: a *fewer* number is incorrect; say a *smaller* number.
>
> *Less* takes a singular noun, *fewer* a plural noun; thus, *less* opportunity, *fewer* opportunities.

LETTERS (FRAMEWORK AND CONSTRUCTION)

The secret of devising the right framework for an official letter lies in finding the right answers to two questions. One is: how am I to start? The other is: to whom am I to attribute the sentiments, opinions and decisions that the letter contains? The old-fashioned full-dress official letter presents no difficulty. That must begin with the traditional " In reply to your letter of . . . I am directed by the Secretary of State for . . . to state for the information of the Lords Commissioners of . . . ". It must continue in the same strain. The signatory must efface his personality. He is nothing; his parliamentary chief is everything. Decisions and opinions must have an introductory " I am to say that . . . " or " the Secretary of State (or for variety Mr. . . . , or for further variety Mr. Secretary . . .) has decided that . . . ". The style is perhaps pompous, but it has the charm of ancient custom, and it is quite easy to learn. It is easy to overdo also, and a warning not to overdo it is the only advice that need be given about it. Do not be too free with its well-starched frills—" I am moreover to observe ", " The Secretary of State cannot conceal from himself ", " I am to ask that you will cause your Minister to be informed "—and all that sort of thing. Even in the traditional field there is a salutary movement towards simplicity.

We find ourselves in more difficult country when we come to new fields of governmental activity, and the correspondence that grows in such profusion there. I mean that part of an official's duty which consists in explaining to members of the public the provisions of the innumerable laws and regulations by which they are protected, guided and restrained. For these the traditional style will not do. Not only is it too stiff, remote and unfriendly, but also it is really too ridiculous to go on pretending that the Ministerial head of the department has been told anything about such letters. Everyone knows that they are sent on the responsibility of one of his subordinates, exercising a delegated authority. A new framework must be devised. Since a wholly satisfactory one has not yet, I believe, been found, it is worth while to examine the problem in some detail.

Everyone's inclination is to follow tradition at least to the point of beginning all replies " In reply to (or ' with reference to ') your letter of . . . " That brings us to our first difficulty. If we are forbidden to follow our natural inclination to continue " I am directed ", as we have seen we must be, how are we to go on?

In detail the possibilities are infinite, but the main forms are few. " I have (or ' I am ') to inform you " used to be—perhaps still is—the most common. But it is unsatisfactory, not to say silly, with its mysterious suggestion of some compulsion working undisclosed in the background. " I would inform you " is another popular variant. It is passable, but not to be commended, for its archaic use of *would* in the sense of " I should like to " makes it stiff, as though one were to say " I would have you know ". " I should inform you ", in the sense of " it is my duty to inform you " is also passable and sometimes useful. But it will not do always ; it is less suitable for beginning than for picking up something at the end (" I should add ", " I should explain however "). " I beg to inform you " will not do. *See* BEG. " I regret to inform you " and " I am glad to inform you " will do nicely when there is anything to be glad or sorry about, but that is not always. " In reply to your letter . . . I wish to inform you " (which I have seen) is crushingly stiff; this also is almost like saying " I would have you know ". The passive (" you are informed ", " it is regretted ", " it is appreciated ") has an impersonal aloofness that ought to rule it out conclusively, but I have noticed that it is common. There remains the device of plunging straight into saying what you have to say without any introductory words. But this will not do as a continuation of " In reply to your letter ". What is in reply to the letter is not the information but the giving of it. It is nonsense to say " In reply to your letter of . . . you have already had all the petrol you are entitled to ", or " In reply to your letter of . . . the Income Tax Law on personal allowances has been changed ".

Must we then conclude that in this type of letter we ought to abandon the stock opening " In reply to your letter " unless we can continue naturally with " I am glad to tell you ", or " I am sorry to have to tell you ", or some such phrase ? Perhaps. Nothing would be lost. There are plenty of other ways of beginning that will not lead us into the same difficulties. The trouble about " In reply to your letter " is that it forms the beginning of a sentence which we must finish somehow. If we turn it into a complete sentence we shake off those shackles.

This must be done with discretion ; some attempts are unfortunate. For instance:

> With reference to your claim. I have to advise you that before same is dealt with . . .

There is no need to start with an ejaculatory and verbless clause. All that was needed was to begin : " Before I can deal with your claim ". (For the misuse of *advise* and *same* in this example *see* ADVISE and SAME.) Or again:

> Your letter is acknowledged, and the following would appear to be the position.
>
> Receipt of your letter is acknowledged. It is pointed out . . .

Here again is the inhuman third person. The right way of saying what these two were trying to say is " Thank you for your letter. The position is (or the facts are) as follows . . . "

I believe that a common opening formula during the war was:

> Your letter of the . . . about . . . We really cannot see our way . . .

I am told that this is fortunately dying out, perhaps because it is becoming less difficult to see our way.

Another not very happy effort is:

> I refer to recent correspondence and to the form which you have completed . . .

There is a faint air of bombast about this: it vaguely recalls Pistol's way of talking (" I speak of Africa and golden joys "). Probably " Thank you for the completed form " would have been an adequate opening.

There are however many possible ways of turning " with reference to your letter " into a complete sentence without getting ourselves into trouble.

> I have received your letter of . . .
>
> Thank you for your letter of . . .
>
> I am writing to you in reply to your letter of . . .
>
> You wrote to me on such-and-such a subject
>
> I have looked into the question of . . . about which you wrote to me

and so on. All enable you to say what you have to say as a direct statement without any preliminary words like " I have to say " or " I would say ".

There remains the second question. To whom are you to attribute the opinions and decisions which, having got over the first hurdle, you then proceed to deliver? In a large and increasing class of letters the answer is simple. These are the letters sent from those provincial offices of a Ministry that are in charge of an official who has a recognised status and title and who signs the letters himself. Such are Inspectors of Taxes, Collectors of Customs, the Regional Controllers of various Departments, Telephone Managers, and others. Everyone knows that these officers exercise a delegated authority; those who draft the letters for them to sign can use the first person, and all is plain sailing.

But a great many letters, sent from other branches of Government Departments, are signed not by someone of known status and authority, but by some unknown person in the hierarchy, who may or may not have consulted higher authority before signing; that is a matter of domestic organisation within the Department and is nobody else's business. To whom are the opinions and decisions conveyed in these letters to be attributed? It cannot be the Minister himself; we have ruled that out. There are four other possibilities. One is that the letter should be written in the first person, and that the official who signs it should boldly accept responsibility, tempered perhaps by the illegibility of his signature. The second is that responsibility should be spread by the use of the first person plural. The third is that it should be further diluted by attributing the decisions and opinions to " the Department ". The fourth is that responsibility should be assigned to a quarter mystically remote by the use throughout of the impersonal passive. To illustrate what I mean, let us take what must today be the most common type of letter, one turning down an application :

> I have considered your application and do not think you have made out a case.
>
> We have considered your application and do not think you have made a case.
>
> The Department has (or have) considered your application and does (or do) not think you have made out a case.
>
> Your application has been considered and it is not thought that you have made out a case.

I cannot pretend to be an authoritative guide on the comparative merits of these; no doubt every Department makes its own rules. But there are three things that seem to me important.

First, in letters written in the first person be very careful to avoid giving the impression that an all-powerful individual is signifying his pleasure. If the letter grants what is asked for, never say that you are making a " concession ". If it refuses a request never say, as in the example given, *I* do not think you have made out a case. Imply that what you have to do is not yourself to be your correspondent's judge, but merely to decide how the case before you fits into the instructions under which you work.

Secondly, it is a mistake to mix these methods in one letter unless there is good reason for it. If you choose an impersonal method, such as " the Department ", you may of course need to introduce the first person for personal purposes such as " I am glad " or " I am sorry " or " I should like you to call here," " I am glad to say that the Department has . . . " But do not mix the methods merely for variety, saying *I* in the first paragraph, *we* in the second, *the Department* in the third, and *it is* in the fourth. Choose one and stick to it.

Thirdly, avoid the impersonal passive, with its formal unsympathetic phrases such as " it is felt ", " it is regretted ", " it is appreciated ". Your correspondent wants to feel that he is dealing with human beings, not with robots. How feeble is the sentence " It is thought you will now have received the form of agreement " compared with " I expect you will have received the form of agreement by now ".

It will be fitting to end this section by giving an example of what seems to me an admirably written letter.

> I thank you for your letter of the 14th October, applying for telephone service F....n 2462 made available by the removal of Mr. X from 25 Station Road. I regret however that owing to the large number of applicants who have prior claims to the line it will not be possible to allow you to take over that telephone installation.
>
> I am sorry to have to give you this decision since I realise just how useful a telephone would be to you.
>
> If you would like to have your name placed on the waiting list for a telephone at 25 Station Road, I shall be glad to have it recorded and to notify you as soon as telephone service can be given.

LIABLE *see* LIKELY

LIKE

Colloquial English admits *like* as a conjunction, and would not be shocked at such a sentence as " Nothing succeeds like success does ". In America they go ever further, and say " It looks like he was going to succeed ". But in English prose neither of these will do. *Like* must not be treated as a conjunction. It must be " regarded as an adjective or adverb having the additional power of directly governing nouns as if it were a preposition " (Fowler). So we may say " nothing succeeds like success " ; but it must be " nothing succeeds *as* success does " and " it looks *as if* he were going to succeed ".

LIKELY

Likely, *liable*, *apt*, *prone* and *calculated* are all used as words denoting probability. They have their different nuances, which should be respected by those who care about treating words in a discriminating way.

Apt and *prone* imply that the probability arises from the disposition of the subject, and usually connote faults or weaknesses. " He is apt to take offence." " She is prone to tears." *Liable* also suggests that the subject is likely to suffer from something prejudicial. " It is liable to break when you put a strain on it." " He is liable to have a fit if you excite him." *Likely* is colourless. Unlike the others, it contains no suggestion of habit but may refer to a single event. Nor does it imply that the probability arises from the subject's disposition ; the probability may be in the nature of things. " Today is likely to be fine." " He is likely to make a success in the job." The suggestion in *calculated* is of judgment in the light of full knowledge ; in the words *not calculated* judgment is passed on an unsuccessful design. "He took elaborate precautions, but they were not of a kind calculated to be successful."

LIMITED

It is pedantry to object to the use of *limited* in the sense of *restricted* on the ground that everything that is not unlimited must be limited. But the word should be used with discretion and should not be allowed to make a writer forget such words as *few* and *small.* Weseen, quoted by Eric Partridge, says :

> *Limited* is not in good use as a substitute for *small* or one of its synonyms. "A man of limited (meagre) education and limited (inadequate) capital is likely to be limited to a limited (scant) income."

LIQUIDATE and LIQUIDATION

Liquidation is the process of ascertaining a debtor's liabilities and apportioning his assets to meet them—winding up his affairs, in fact. The meaning has lately been enlarged so as to signify other sorts of winding-up, especially, with a sinister twist, the removal of opposition in a totalitarian state by methods possibly undisclosed but certainly unpleasant. The reason for this extension is no doubt to be found in the extension of the practices for which it stands. There are some who deprecate this enlargement of the word's meaning, but I do not think there is any use in doing that; it is well established, and can justly claim to be expressive and vivid and to fill a need. Mr. Churchill uses it in *The Gathering Storm:*

> Many of the ordinary guarantees of civilised society had been already liquidated by the Communist pervasion of the decayed Parliamentary Government.

The mischief is that liquidate is one of the words, which, having once broken out, run wild. The far-fetched word *terminate*, having superseded the familiar *end*, is itself being superseded by the more far-fetched *liquidate.* It is now apparently regarded as suitable for denoting the ending of anything from massacring a nation to giving an employee notice. It should therefore be handled with care.

LITERALLY

Avoid the foolish use of *literally* in a sense that really means "not literally but metaphorically", e.g. "He literally brought the house down", "I am literally snowed under with work".

This perennial recently flowered in the correspondence columns of *The Times.* Among the choicer blossoms were:

(In an account of a tennis match) Miss X literally wiped the floor with her opponent.

(A comment by *Punch* on a statement in a newspaper that throughout a certain debate Mr. Gladstone had sat "literally glued to the Treasury Bench") "That's torn it" said the grand old man, as he literally wrenched himself away to dinner.

(Of a certain horse) It literally ran away with the Two Thousand Guineas.

(Of a rackets player) He literally blasted his opponent out of the court.

M. Clemenceau literally exploded during the argument.

He literally died in harness.

LOAN

Present-day taste in this country prefers the verb *lend*, confining *loan* to the duties of a noun. *Loan* as a verb went to America with the Pilgrim Fathers and settled there; it is now trying to come back again, but we have done without it for so long that we look on it as something of an outsider.

LOCATE and LOCATION

These words have their proper uses. "The United Nations Organisation is located at Lake Success." "I do not know the location of my unit." Those are proper uses. But the words are often used where simpler words would do as well or better—*find* for the verb and *place* or *position* for the noun.

By an unfortunate oversight the file was mislaid, and it was not until the receipt of your letter that a thorough search was made and the file located.

Located does not mitigate the offence any more than a blunt *found* would have done.

MAJOR

This is a harmless word, but it is so much used that it is supplanting other more serviceable ones. Do not use *major* where you might use such a word as *main*, *important*, *chief*, *principal*. For instance *important* or *significant* would have been better than *major* in:

We do not expect to see any major change in the near future.

MAJORITY

The major part, and *the majority* ought not to be used when a plain *most* would meet the case. They should be reserved for occasions when the difference between a majority and a minority is significant. Thus:

Most of the members have been slack in their attendance.

The majority of members are likely to be against the proposal.

When the word is used in an abstract sense it should have a singular verb (" a two-thirds majority is necessary ") ; where it denotes the people composing the majority the verb should be plural (" a majority of the committee were against the proposal ").

MANY A

Many a always takes a singular verb. " There's many a slip twixt cup and lip " is idiomatic English.

MATERIALISE

Do not use this showy word, or the similar word *eventuate* (*see* EVENTUATE) when a simpler one would do as well or better, e.g. *happen*, *occur*, *come about*, *take place*, or even the colloquial *come off*.

> It was thought at the time that the incoming tenant would take over the fixtures. This did not however materialise. (. . . But he did not.)

Materialise has its own work to do as a transitive verb in the sense of investing something non-material with material attributes, and as an intransitive verb in the sense of appearing in bodily form.

MEANS

Means in the sense of " means to an end " is a curious word ; it may be treated either as singular or as plural. Supposing for instance that you wanted to say that means had been sought to do something, you may if you choose treat the word as singular and say " a means was sought " or " every means was sought ". Or you may treat it as plural and say " all means were sought ". Or again, if you use just the word *means* without any word such as *a* or *every* or *all* to show its number, you may give it a singular or plural verb as you wish : you may say either " means was sought " or " means were sought " ; both are idiomatic. Perhaps on the whole it is best to say " a method (or way) was sought " if there was only one, and " means were sought " if there was more than one.

Means in the sense of monetary resources is always plural.

MEANTIME and MEANWHILE

In modern usage *meanwhile* is certainly an adverb and *meantime* preferably a noun. You may say *meanwhile* or *in the meantime*: not *in the meanwhile* and preferably not *meantime* by itself.

METAPHOR

Metaphors are invaluable devices. They enable a writer to convey ideas briefly and vividly that might otherwise need pages of tedious exposition. What would become of us, in our present economic straits, without our *targets*, *ceilings*, *blueprints*, and *bottlenecks*? *See* TARGET, CEILING, BOTTLENECK. But metaphors are not without their dangers. Here are two.

One is that they are so attractive, especially when new. They sparkle like gems. They seem to say in a word just what we are trying laboriously to put across. It may be moreover that we are rather proud to have learned a new one, and want to show off. Thus new metaphors tend to be used indiscriminately and soon get stale, but not before they have elbowed out words perhaps more commonplace but with meanings more precise. Sometimes metaphors are so absurdly overtaxed that they become a laughing-stock and die of ridicule. That has been the fate of " exploring every avenue " and of " leaving no stone unturned ". *See* CLICHÉ.

Another danger in the use of metaphors is of falling into incongruity. So long at least as they are " live "* metaphors, they must not be given a context that would be absurd if the words used metaphorically were being used literally. We must not refer to the biggest bottleneck when what we mean is the most troublesome one for that will obviously be the narrowest. We must not speak of " sterilising " land when what we mean is that it is to be left unbuilt on in order that it may continue to give us the fruits of the earth. We must not speak of " extending " a ceiling when what we mean is raising it. The statesman who said that sections of the population were being squeezed flat by inflation was not then in his happiest vein, nor was the writer who claimed for American sociology the distinction of having always immersed itself in concrete situations. We cannot but admit that there is no hope of checking the astonishing antics of *target* and of bringing that flighty word within reasonable bounds. *See* TARGET. But do not let us have any more metaphors getting out of hand like that.

METICULOUS

Meticulous is derived from a Latin word meaning timid, and like its plebeian cousin *pernickety*, still retains a flavour of fussiness over

*A live metaphor is one that evokes in the reader a mental picture of the imagery of its origin ; a dead one does not. If we write " the situation is in hand " and " he has taken the bit between his teeth ", we are in both going to horsemanship for our metaphor. But to most readers the first would be a dead metaphor, and the sentence would have no different impact from " the situation is under control "; the second would be a live one, calling up, however faintly and momentarily, the picture of a runaway horse.

trifles. It should only be used where the writer wants to emphasise that carefulness is overdone; it should not be treated as a synonym for *scrupulous* or any other commendatory word.

MORE THAN ONE

This phrase takes illogically a singular verb, no doubt owing to the pull of the singular *one*. Write: " More than one question was (not were) asked ".

MULTILATERAL *see* UNILATERAL

MUTUAL

For a long time a battle has been carried on between those who say that it is improper to use *mutual* in the sense of " pertaining to both parties ", " common ", as in the phrase " Our mutual friend ", and those who, like Dickens, insist on so using it. The O.E.D. says that this usage goes back to the sixteenth century, but that " it is now regarded as incorrect ". Possibly the reason why it persists so stubbornly is the ambiguity of " common ". " They have common ancestors " may be misunderstood. While the battle is undecided the prudent writer will confine his use of *mutual* to the universally accepted meaning of *reciprocal* (as in " mutual admiration society ") and will so avoid the risk of giving offence or being thought ignorant.

NEGATIVE (DOUBLE NEGATIVE)

It has long been settled doctrine among English grammarians that two negatives cancel each other and produce an affirmative. Just as in mathematics $-(-x)$ equals $+x$, so in language " he did not say nothing " must be regarded as equivalent to " he said something ".

It is going too far to say, as is sometimes said, that this proposition is self-evident. The Greeks did not think that two negatives made an affirmative. On the contrary, the more negatives they put into a sentence the more emphatically negative the sentence became. Nor did Chaucer think so, for, in a much-quoted passage, he wrote:

> He never yit no vileineye ne sayde
> In al his lyf, unto no maner wight
> He was a verray parfit gentil knyght.

Nor did Shakespeare, who made King Claudius say:

> Nor what he said, though it lacked form a little,
> Was not like madness.

Nor do the many thousands of people who find it natural today to deny knowledge by saying " I don't know nothing at all about it ". And the comedian who sings " I ain't going to give nobody none of mine " is not misunderstood.

> Such repeated negatives, says Jespersen, are usual in a great many languages in which the negative element is comparatively small in phonetic bulk, and is easily attracted to various words. If the negation were expressed once only, it might easily be overlooked ; hence the speaker, who wants the negative sense to be fully appreciated, attaches it not only to the verb, but also to other parts of the sentence : he spreads, as it were, a thin layer of negative colouring over the whole of the sentence instead of confining it to one single place. This may be called pleonastic, but is certainly not really illogical.

Still, the grammarians' rule should be observed in English today. Breaches of it are commonest with verbs of surprise or speculation (" I shouldn't wonder if there wasn't a storm ". " I shouldn't be surprised if he didn't come today "). Indeed this is so common that it is classed by Fowler among his " sturdy indefensibles ". A recent speech in the House of Lords affords a typical instance of the confusion of thought bred by double negatives:

> Let it not be supposed because we are building for the future rather than the present that the Bill's proposals are not devoid of significance.

What the speaker meant, of course, was " Let it not be supposed that the bill's proposals *are* devoid of significance ".

Another example is:

> There is no reason to doubt that what he says in his statement . . . is not true.

Here the speaker meant, " There is no reason to doubt that his statement *is* true ".

And another:

> It must not be assumed that there are no circumstances in which a profit might not be made.

Always avoid multiple negatives when you can. Even if you dodge the traps they set and succeed in saying what you mean, you give your reader a puzzle to solve in sorting the negatives out.

NEITHER . . . NOR

Some books tell you that *neither . . . nor* should not be used where the alternatives are more than two. But if you decide to ignore this advice as pedantry you will find on your side not only the translators of the Bible,

> Neither death, nor life, nor angels, nor principalities, nor powers, nor things present, nor things to come, nor height, nor depth, nor any other creature, shall be able to separate us from the love of God,

but also, though not quite so profusely, Mr. Harold Nicolson,

> Neither Lord Davidson nor Sir Bernard Paget nor Mr. Arthur Bryant will suffer permanently from the spectacle which they have provided.

See also NOR.

NEW VERBS

These are great days for new verbs. They multiply and flourish exceedingly. Perhaps this is partly due to the importance of advertisement in modern life; a new and snappy verb will catch the eye where an old one would go unnoticed. The paper shortage, and the hurry in which we all live, may also have something to do with it, for the apparent purpose of some of these new verbs is to say in one word what would otherwise need two or three.

New verbs are ordinarily formed in one of three ways, all of which have in the past been used to create acceptable additions to our vocabulary. One is the simple method of treating a noun as if it were a verb. This was the origin of the verb *question*, and of many others. The second is to add *ise* to an adjective, as *sterilise* has been formed from *sterile*. The third is by what is called " back-formation ", that is to say forming from a noun the sort of verb from which the noun might have been formed if the verb had come first. In this way the verb *diagnose* was formed from the noun *diagnosis*.

The following are some of the words whose growing popularity is presumably due to our wish to make a single word serve for two or three:

To audition (to give an audition to).
To contact (to make contact with).
To donate (to make a donation of).
To enthuse (to be enthusiastic).
To feature (to make a prominent feature of).
To finalise (to put into final form).
To glimpse (to catch a glimpse of).
To hospitalise (to send to hospital).
To message (to send a message to).
To position (to put into position).
To publicise (to give publicity to).
To reposition (to put back into position).
To sense (to become vaguely aware of).
To site (to choose a site for).

These are generally regarded as new verbs, though the truth is that several of them are words of respectable antiquity dug out of an oblivion in which some may think they might well have remained. Only five of them are not included in the *Shorter Oxford English Dictionary* published in 1933—*audition*, *finalise*, *hospitalise*, *publicise* and *reposition*. *Contact* is said to be " rare, technical ", *donate* to be " chiefly U.S.", and *enthuse* to be " U.S. slang ". The rest are recognised without comment as verbs.

Even if it were true that these verbs make it possible to express in one word what would otherwise need several—and in some cases this is arguable—that would not necessarily be a justification for trying to force into the language verbs as unpleasant as some of these are. All of them, except perhaps *site* (but *see also* CONTACT), may still give offence to some readers, and therefore should not be used by official writers; their duty is to follow recognised usage, not to innovate*. The ultimate fate of these words depends not on the verdict of any individual but on popular opinion, which decides these questions in the long run, generally with good sense.

Still more is it the duty of all self-respecting writers to refrain from using those new verbs that are formed by pretending that a noun is a verb and using it in exactly the same sense as an existing genuine verb. Examples of these are *architect* for *design*, *author* for *write*, *decision* for *decide*, *gift* for *give*, *signature* for *sign*, *suspicion* for *suspect*. None of these is tolerable.

Other verbs base their claims on the plea that they represent something new, or if not actually new, something which is so much more in evidence than it used to be that a new word for it is justified. Among these are *decontaminate*, *derestrict* (*see* DE and DIS), *pressurise*, *rationalise*, *recondition*, *rehabilitate*, *sabotage* and *service* (*see* SABOTAGE and SERVICE). All these have a good footing and none is likely to be driven out, much as some people may regret it.

NON

A warning has already been given against creating new words by prefixing *dis* to old ones. *See* DE and DIS. The same warning is needed about *non*. A suitable opposite probably already exists. " Institutions for the care of the non-sick " does not strike the reader as a felicitous title. *Non-sick* is presumably intended to mean something different from healthy, but if so the difference should be explained; it is not apparent. Some words have created their opposites in this way. Such are *non-appearance*, *non-combatant*, *non-conformist*, *non-existent*, and others. But the lazy habit of using *non* to turn any word upside-down so as not to have the

---

*Perhaps Government advertisements are different. *See* POSITION.

trouble of thinking of its proper opposite is becoming sadly common. Sir Alan Herbert remarked some years ago that no one would think of saying *non-sober* when he meant *drunk*. I cannot feel sure that that is still true.

I should have said that this trick was of quite recent origin if Mr. G. M. Young had not sent me an eighty-year-old example of it that would hold its own against any modern rival. Sir John Simon, F.R.S., the eminent surgeon who later became a government official, giving evidence before the Royal Commission on the Sanitary Laws in 1869, referred to " a disease hereditarily transmissible and spreading among the non-fornicative part of the population ". Mr. Young says he was surprised to come across this, because Simon was a man of culture and a friend of Ruskin. " It just shows ", he adds unkindly, " what Whitehall can do ".

NONE

None may be used indifferently with a singular or a plural verb. The plural used to be commoner, but the singular has been catching up recently, probably under the mistaken impression that it is more correct because it is more logical. *See* SINGULAR and PLURAL.

NOR and OR

When should *nor* be used and when *or*? If a *neither* or an *either* comes first there is no difficulty ; *neither* is always followed by *nor* and *either* by *or*. There can be no doubt that it is wrong to write " The existing position satisfies neither the psychologist, the judge, or the public ". It should have been " neither the psychologist, nor the judge, nor the public ". But when the initial negative is a simple *not* or *no*, it is often a puzzling question whether *nor* or *or* should follow. Logically it depends on whether the sentence is so framed that the initial negative runs on into the second part of it or is exhausted in the first ; practically it may be of little importance which answer you give, for the meaning will be clear.

> He did not think that the Bill would be introduced this month, nor indeed before the recess.

" He did not think " affects every thing that follows *that*. Logically therefore *nor* produces a double negative, as though one were to say " he didn't think it wouldn't be introduced before the recess ".

> The blame for this disorder does not rest with Parliament, or with the bishops, or with the parish priests. Our real weakness is the failure of the ordinary man.

Here the negative phrase " does not rest " is carried right through the sentence, and applies to the bishops and the parish priests as much as to Parliament. There is no need to repeat the negative, and *or* is logically right. But *nor* is so often used in such a construction that it would be pedantic to condemn it : if logical defence is needed one might say that " did he think it would be introduced " in the first example, and " does it rest " in the second were understood as repeated after *nor.* But if the framework of the sentence is changed to :

> The blame for this disorder rests not with Parliament nor with the bishops, nor with the parish priests, but with the ordinary man,

it is a positive verb (*rests*) that runs through the sentence ; the original negative (*not*) is attached not to the verb but to *Parliament*, and exhausts itself in exonerating Parliament. The negative must be repeated, and *nor* is rightly used.

NOT

(*a*) " Not all ".

It is idiomatic English, to which no exception can be taken, to write " all officials are not good draftsmen " when you mean that only some of them are. Compare "All that glitters is not gold ". But it is clearer, and therefore better, to write " Not all officials are good draftsmen ".

(*b*) " Not . . . but ".

It is also idiomatic English to write " I did not go to speak but to listen ". It is pedantry to insist that, because logic demands it, this ought to be " I went not to speak but to listen ". But if the latter way of arranging a " not . . . but " sentence runs as easily and makes your meaning clearer, as it often may, it should be preferred.

See Because.

For double negative, *see* Negative.

NOUN ADJECTIVES

The English language has been greatly enriched by its readiness to treat nouns as adjectives. We are surrounded by innumerable examples—*War Department*, *Highway Code*, *Nursery School*, *Weather Forecast*, *Trades Union Congress*, and so on. But something has gone wrong recently with this useful practice. It is shockingly abused in newspaper headlines, and this has set up a corruption that is poisoning English prose. It seems to be natural today to write clodhopping stuff like " World population is increasing faster than world food production " instead of " The population of the world is increasing faster than the food it produces ". Lord Dunsany has described this process :

> Too many *ofs* have dropped out of the language, and the dark of the floor is littered with this useful word. Only the other day I was puzzled by a reference in *The Times* to " valuable type specimens ". What, I wondered, are type specimens. But I worked out that it meant specimens of valuable types. . . . My friend, the late Mr. Anthony Crossley, once told me, when I was talking on this subject, of a heading he had found in a paper which went :
>
> Sir John Simon and Car Chase Widow.
>
> I remember most clearly that it was no reflection whatever upon Sir John Simon, as he was then, or even upon his car, or his chauffeur ; but what it did mean, though Mr. Crossley told me at the time, I cannot remember, and I shall never know now, for there is no making head or tail of the words themselves. Far worse than the examples I have quoted are to be met with daily, things like " England side captain selection " instead of " Selection of captain of English eleven " ; or even " England side captain selection difficulty ". Nor would they stop nowadays at " England side captain selection difficulty rumour ".

This sort of language is no doubt pardonable in headlines, where as many stimulating words as possible must be crowded into spaces so small that *treaties* have had to become *pacts*, *ambassadors envoys*, and *investigations probes*. Headlines have become a language of their own, knowing no law and often quite incomprehensible until one has read the article that they profess to summarise. " INSANITY RULES CRITIC " and " W. H. SMITH OFFER SUCCESS " have quite different meanings from their apparent ones. Who could know what is meant by " HANGING PROBE NAMES SOON " until he has read on and discovered that what it means is " The names of the members of the Royal Commission on Capital Punishment will shortly be announced " ?

But what may be pardonable in headlines will not do in the text. For instance:

> Rationing of meat must continue because of the world supply situation (because there is not enough meat in the world).

An exceptionally choice example is:

> On the basis of the present head of labour ceiling allocation overall.

Here *Head of labour* means *number of building operatives*. *Ceiling* means *maximum*. *Overall*, as usual, means nothing. The whole sentence means " If we get the maximum number of building operatives at present allotted to us ". *See* CEILING and OVERALL.

> Everything is being done to expedite plant installation within the limiting factors of steel availability and the preparation of sites.

The only thing that can be said for the writer of this is that his conscience pulled him up before the end, and he did not write " sites preparation ". The sentence should have run " So far as steel is available and sites can be prepared, everything is being done to expedite the installation of plant ".

The use of a noun as an adjective should be avoided where the same word is already an adjective with a different meaning. Do not, for instance, say " material allocation " when you mean " allocation of material ", but reserve that expression against the time when you may want to make clear that the allocation you are considering is not a spiritual one.

For the same reason this phrase is not felicitous:

> In view of the restrictions recently imposed on our capital economic situation . . .

NUMBER

(i) Like other collective nouns, *number* may take either a singular or a plural verb. Unlike most of them, it admits of a simple and logical rule. When all that it is doing is forming part of a composite plural subject, it should have a plural verb, as in:

> A large number of people are coming today.

But when it is standing on its own legs as the subject it should have a singular verb, as in:

> The number of people coming today is large.

The following are accordingly unidiomatic:

> There is a number of applications, some of which were made before yours.
>
> There is a large number of outstanding orders.

The true subjects are not " a number " and " a large number " but "a-number-of-applications" and "a-large-number-of-outstanding-orders ". *Is* should therefore be *are* in each.

Of the following examples the first has a singular verb that should be plural and the second a plural verb that should be singular.

> There was also a number of conferences calling themselves peace conferences which had no real interest in peace.
>
> The number of casualties in H.M.S. *Amethyst* are thought to be about fifteen.

(ii) There is no point in writing *a number of* when what you mean is *some*, *several*, or *many*; you merely use three words where one is enough.

OCCASION

Do not use *occasion* as a verb when a simpler word such as *cause* would do as well. It is a stilted verb.

Any inconvenience occasioned is regretted.

I am sorry for any inconvenience occasioned to you by this inadvertency.

The word seems to be treated in official letters as the natural partner of *inconvenience*, and it is always a bad sign when one word invariably suggests another. (*Alternative accommodation*, *real danger* and *active consideration* are examples.) There are plenty of other verbs with much the same meaning, and they should be given their innings. " Any inconvenience you have suffered." " Any inconvenience you may have been caused." " Any inconvenience you have been put to." Any of these will do for a change.

The person to whom the inconvenience is " occasioned " need not always be described as " experiencing " it. *See* EXPERIENCE.

ONE

(i) Unlike *its*, *hers*, *ours*, *yours* and *theirs*, the possessive of *one* is *one's* not *ones*.

(ii) *One* has a way of intruding in such a sentence as " The problem is not an easy one ". " The problem is not easy " may be a neater way of saying what you mean.

(iii) What pronoun should be used with *one*? *His* or *one's*, for example? That depends on what sort of a *one* it is, whether " numeral " or " impersonal ", to use Fowler's labels. Fowler illustrates the difference thus :

One hates *his* enemies and another forgives them (numeral).

One hates *one's* enemies and loves *one's* friends (impersonal).

(iv) " One of those who . . . " A common error in sentences of this sort is to use a singular verb instead of a plural, as though the antecedent of *who* were *one* and not *those*—to write for instance : " It is one of the exceptional cases that calls for (instead of call for) exceptional treatment ".

(v) Avoid the construction " One of the most difficult, if not the most difficult, cases . . . " Neither *case* nor *cases* sounds right. Write " one of the most difficult cases, if not the most difficult ".

ONLY

The correct place for *only*, as for other adverbs, is next to (preferably immediately before) the word it qualifies. But *only* is a wayward word. It is much given to deserting its post and taking its place next the verb, regardless of what it qualifies. It is more natural to say " he only spoke for ten minutes " than

" he spoke for only ten minutes ". The sport of pillorying misplaced *onlys* has a great fascination for some people, and opportunity for indulging in it is never far away. A recent book, devoted to the exposing of errors of diction in contemporary writers, contained several examples such as:

> He had only been in England for six weeks since the beginning of the war.
>
> This only makes a war lawful: that it is a struggle for Law against Force.
>
> We can only analyse the facts we all have before us.

These incur the author's censure. By the same reasoning he would condemn Mr. Churchill for writing in *The Gathering Storm:*

> Statesmen are not called upon only to settle easy questions.

Fowler took a different view. Of a critic who protested against " he only died a week ago " instead of " he died only a week ago " Fowler wrote:

> There speaks one of those friends from whom the English language may well pray to be saved, one of the modern precisians who have more zeal than discretion . . .

So do not take too seriously those I have elsewhere called " the only-snoopers ". But be on the alert. It will generally be safe to put *only* in what the plain man feels to be its natural place. Sometimes that will be its logical position, sometimes not. Sometimes a natural but ungrammatical position is a positive aid to being understood; it prevents the reader from being put on a wrong scent. In the sentence " The temperature will rise above 35 degrees only in the south-west of England ", *only* is carefully put in its right logical place. But the listener would have grasped more quickly the picture of an almost universally cold England if the announcer had said " the temperature will only rise above 35 degrees in the south-west of England ".

A purist might condemn:

> I am to express regret that it has only been possible to issue a licence for part of the quantity for which application was made,

but the ordinary reader will think that this conveys the writer's meaning more readily and naturally than:

> I am to express regret that it has been possible to issue a licence for only part of the quantity for which application was made.

But it cannot be denied that the irresponsible behaviour of *only* does sometimes create real ambiguity. Take such a sentence as:

> His disease can only be alleviated by a surgical operation.

We cannot tell what this means, and must rewrite it either:

> Only a surgical operation can alleviate his disease (it cannot be alleviated in any other way),

or:

> A surgical operation can only alleviate his disease (it cannot cure it).

Again:

> In your second paragraph you point out that carpet-yarn only can be obtained from India, and this is quite correct.

The writer must have meant " can be obtained only from India ", and ought to have so written, or, at the least, " can only be obtained from India ". What he did write, if not actually ambiguous (for it can hardly be supposed that carpet-yarn is India's only product), is unnatural, and sets the reader puzzling for a moment.

OPTIMISTIC

Optimism is the quality of being disposed in all circumstances to hope for the best. The edge of the meaning of *optimistic* is being blunted by its being habitually used for *sanguine*, *hopeful*, and *cheerful*, when what is referred to is not a habit of mind, but an attitude towards particular circumstances.

An example of its unsuitable use is " I will submit your application to the Board, but I am not optimistic about the result ".

OPTIMUM

Do not use *optimum* merely as a showy synonym for *best*. It should only be used of the resultant of conflicting forces. The optimum speed of a motor car is not the fastest it is capable of, but that which reconciles in the most satisfactory way the conflicting desires of its owner to move quickly, to economise petrol, and to avoid needless wear and tear.

ORAL *see* VERBAL

ORDER (IN ORDER THAT)

May or *might* are the words to follow " in order that ". Do not write " in order that no further delay will occur " or " in order that we can have a talk on the subject ".

OTHERWISE

Twenty years ago Fowler pointed out that this word was having " very curious experiences " in that, although an adverb, it was being used more and more both as an adjective and as a noun. These experiences have certainly not abated since then.

The adjective that *otherwise* dispossesses is *other*. This is exemplified in such a sentence as " There are many difficulties, legal and otherwise, about doing what you ask ".

The noun that *otherwise* dispossesses is whatever noun has the contrary meaning to one just mentioned. This is exemplified in such a sentence as " I will say nothing about the reasonableness or otherwise of what you ask ", where the word replaced is *unreasonableness*.

Fowler condemns both these as ungrammatical. Since it is just as easy in the first case to write *other* and in the second either to omit *or otherwise* or to substitute the appropriate noun, there is no reason why one should not be on the safe side and do the grammatical thing. But it would be wrong to leave the subject without quoting Dr. Ballard:

> A new pronoun is as rare a phenomenon as a new comet. Yet it dawned on me the other day that a new pronoun had insidiously crept into the English language. It was heard on everybody's lips, it was used on the platform and in the Press, it figured prominently in blue-books and official papers. And yet I could find it in no dictionary—not, that is, as a pronoun—nor could I discover it among the lists of pronouns in any grammar, however modern. Still, if the current definition is correct, the word is beyond doubt a pronoun. The word is *otherwise*. A committee is appointed by an educational body *to report on the success or otherwise of the new organisation of schools*. What does *otherwise* stand for? Why *failure*, of course. And *failure* is a noun. Therefore *otherwise* is a pronoun. . . . I thought at first with Mr. H. W. Fowler that *otherwise*, so used, was not a pronoun but a blunder. But when I considered the people who used it so—schoolmasters and school inspectors, and ambassadors, and statesmen and judges on the bench—I could not accept Mr. Fowler's views. For I would rather wrong the dead—dead languages that is—and wrong myself and you than I would wrong such honourable men. There is no help for it. *Otherwise* is a pronoun.

Sometimes *other* gets its revenge, and supplants *otherwise*.

> It is news to me that a sheep improves the land other than by the food fed through it.

OVERALL (adjective)

The favour that this word has won during the past few years is astonishing. It is an egregious example of the habit of preferring a novel word of vague import to established words of precise meaning ; indeed this word seems to have a quality that impels people to use it in settings in which it has no meaning at all.

Examples of its meaningless use are:

> The independence of the Teaching Hospitals and their freedom from the overall control of the Regional Boards . . . .

The overall growth of London should be restrained.

Radical changes will be necessary in the general scheme of exchequer grants in aid of local authorities, therefore, to secure that overall the policy of the Government in concentrating those grants as far as possible where the need is greatest is further developed. (Here, it will be observed, *overall* is an adverb.)

When an individual leaves an establishment, and his departure results in a net reduction of one in the overall strength . . .

It looks as if the yield for the first fortnight of 1949 will be fewer than forty fresh orders, representing an overall annual output of no more than a thousand.

When *overall* is not meaningless, it is commonly used as a synonym for some more familiar word, especially *average*, *total*, and *aggregate*.

For *aggregate:*

Compared with the same week a year ago, overall production of coal showed an increase of more than 100,000 tons. (i.e. deep-mined plus opencast.)

For *in all* or *altogether :*

Overall the broadcasting of " Faust " will cover eight hours.

For *total :*

I have made a note of the overall demand of this company for the next year.

For *average :*

The houses here are built to an overall density of three to the acre.

For *supreme :*

Vice-Admiral Duncan, of the United States Navy, was in overall command.

For *on the whole :*

The Secretary of State for the Colonies stated that the overall position in Malaya had greatly improved, although in some places it was still difficult.

For *generally:*

Small vital schemes of repair and adaptation which continually arise and must be dealt with irrespective of any attempt to improve overall hospital standards.

For *overriding :*

They came forward as witnesses because of the overall fear of being involved in a capital charge.

For *comprehensive :*

An overall plan for North Atlantic Defence measures was approved yesterday by the Defence Minister at the Hague.

For *whole :*

Mr. C. said he could quite understand that the Conservative Party were unwilling to look at the overall picture.

Overall, according to the dictionaries, means " including every thing between the extreme points ", as one speaks of the overall length of a ship. For this purpose it is useful, but it is high time that its excursions into the fields of other words were checked. So ubiquitous has the word become that it is a pleasant surprise to come across an old-fashioned *general* in such sentences as :

> These reports may be used for obtaining a general picture of the efficiency of a given industry.
>
> Although Europe's general deficit with the outside world fell by over $2 billion during 1949, its deficit with the United States fell hardly at all.

Most writers today would say " overall picture " and " overall deficit " almost automatically.

OVERLAPPING

By this I mean a particular form of what the grammarians call *pleonasm*, or *redundancy*. Possible varieties are infinite, but the commonest example is writing " the reason for this is because . . . " instead of either " this is because " or " the reason for this is that . . . " as in the first of these examples.

> The Ministry of Food say that the reason for the higher price of the biscuits is because the cost of chocolate has increased.
>
> The subject of the talk tonight will be about . . . (A confusion between " the subject will be . . ." and " the talk will be about ".)
>
> The reason for the long delay appears to be due to the fact that the medical certificates went astray. (A confusion between " the reason is that the certificates went astray " and " the delay is due to the fact that the certificates went astray ".)
>
> The cause of the delay is due to the shortage of materials. (A confusion between " the cause of the delay is the shortage " and " the delay is due to the shortage ".)
>
> By far the greater majority . . . (A confusion between " the great majority " and " by far the greater part ".)
>
> He did not say that all actions for libel or slander were never properly brought. (A confusion between " that all actions . . . were improperly brought " and " that actions . . . were never properly brought ".)
>
> An attempt will be made this morning to try to avert the threatened strike. (Those who were going to do this might have attempted to do it or tried to do it. But merely to attempt to try seems rather half-hearted.)
>
> Save only in exceptional circumstances will any further development be contemplated. (A confusion between " only in exceptional circumstances will any further development be contemplated " and " save in exceptional circumstances no further development will be contemplated ".)

The common fault of duplicating either the future or the past is a form of this error.

> The most probable thing will be that they will be sold in a government auction.

This should be " The most probable thing is that they will be ".

> The Minister said he would have liked the Government of Eire to have offered us butter instead of cream.

This should be " he would have liked the Government of Eire to offer . . . ".

PADDING

Mr. Winston Churchill when Prime Minister issued a memorandum which said:

> Let us have an end of such phrases as these: " It is also of importance to bear in mind the following considerations . . ." or " consideration should be given to the possibility of carrying into effect . . ." Most of these woolly phrases are mere padding, which can be left out altogether, or replaced by a single word. Let us not shrink from using the short expressive phrase even if it is conversational.

" Padding " then in the sense in which Mr. Churchill used the word consists of clumsy and obtrusive stitches on what ought to be a smooth fabric of consecutive thought. No doubt it comes partly from a feeling that wordiness is an ingredient of politeness, and blunt statement is crude, if not rude. There is an element of truth in this: an over-staccato style is as irritating as an over-sostenuto one. But it is a matter of degree; and official prose is of the sort that calls for plainness rather than elegance. Moreover the habit of " padding " springs partly from less meritorious notions—that the dignity of an official's calling demands a certain verbosity, and that naked truth is indecent and should be clothed in wrappings of woolly words.

Certain clichés that are favourites with padders are dealt with under their own headings in this book, e.g. APPRECIATE, CONNEXION, INFORMATION. Here are added a few miscellaneous examples. In each the words that cannot escape a charge of being mere padding are italicised.

> I am in receipt of your letter of the 4th December, and *for your information* the following extract from regulations under the Act is quoted *for your benefit*. . . .

> I am prepared to accept the discharge of this account by payment in instalments, but *it should be pointed out that* no further service can be allowed until the account is again in credit.

> *The opportunity is taken to mention that* it is understood . . .

> I regret that the wrong form was forwarded. *In the circumstances* I am forwarding a superseding one.
>
> *It should be noted that* there is a possibility of a further sale.
>
> It has been ascertained that Mr. X has kindly consented to share his telephone with you. *In this connexion therefore* I have pleasure in enclosing *herewith* the necessary agreement.

An example of padding of this sort is the precautionary phrase that so often opens every new paragraph of a formal official letter : " I am to add ", " I am further to observe ", " I am moreover to remark ", " finally I am to point out ", and so forth.

PARAGRAPHING

Letters, reports, memoranda and other documents would be unreadable if they were not divided into paragraphs, and much has been written on the art of paragraphing. But little of it helps the ordinary writer ; the subject does not admit of precise guidance. The chief thing to remember is that, although paragraphing loses all point if the paragraphs are excessively long, the paragraph is essentially a unit of thought, not of length. Every paragraph must be homogeneous in subject-matter, and sequential in treatment of it. If a single sequence of treatment of a single subject goes on so long as to make an unreasonably long paragraph, it may be divided into more than one. But you must not do the opposite, and combine into a single paragraph passages that have not this sort of unity, even though each by itself may be below the average length of a paragraph.

PARENTHESIS

The purpose of a parenthesis is ordinarily to insert an illustration, explanation, definition, or additional piece of information of any sort, into a sentence that is logically and grammatically complete without it. A parenthesis may be marked off by commas, dashes or brackets. The degree of interruption of the main sentence may vary from the almost imperceptible one of explanatory words in apposition :

> Mr. Smith, the secretary, read the minutes,

to the violent one of a separate sentence complete in itself :

> A memorandum (six copies of this memorandum are enclosed for the information of the Board) has been issued to management committees.

Parentheses should be used sparingly. Their very convenience is a reason for fighting shy of them. They enable the writer to dodge the trouble of arranging his thought properly ; but he does so at the expense of the reader, especially if the thought that he has spatchcocked into the sentence is an abrupt break in it, or a long one, or both. The second of the two examples just given shows an illegitimate use of the parenthesis. The writer had no business to keep the reader waiting for the verb by throwing in a parenthesis that would have been more appropriate in a separate sentence. The following examples are even worse:

> . . . to regard day nurseries and daily guardians as supplements to meet the special needs (where these exist and cannot be met within the hours, age, range and organisation of nursery schools and nursery classes) of children whose mothers are constrained by individual circumstances to go out to work. . . .

> If duties are however declined in this way, it will be necessary for the Board to consider whether it should agree to a modified contract in the particular case, or whether—because the required service can be provided only by the acceptance of the rejected obligations (e.g. by a whole-time radiologist to perform radiological examinations of paying patients in Section 5 beds in a hospital where the radiologists are all whole-time officers)—the Board should seek the services of another practitioner. . . .

These are intolerable abuses of the parenthesis, the first with its interposition of 21 words in the middle of the phrase " needs of children ", and the second with its double parenthesis, more than 40 words long, like two snakes eating each other. There was no need for either of these monstrosities. In both examples the main sentence should be allowed to finish without interruption, and what is now in the parenthesis, so far as it is worth saying, should be added at the end:

> . . . to regard day nurseries and daily guardians as supplements to meet the special needs of children whose mothers are constrained . . . and whose needs cannot be met. . . .

> . . . or whether the Board should seek the services of another practitioner, as they will have to do if the required service can be provided only . . .

Here is a parenthesis that keeps the reader waiting so long for the verb that he has probably forgotten what the subject is:

> Close affiliation with University research in haematology—and it may be desirable that ultimately each Regional Transfusion Officer should have an honorary appointment in the department of pathology in the medical school—will help to attract into the service medical men of good professional standing.

In former days, when long and involved periods were fashionable, it was customary after a long parenthesis to put the reader on the road again by repeating the subject with the words " I say ". Thus the writer of the last example would have continued after " medical school " with the words " close affiliation with University research in haematology, I say, will help to attract, etc." Now that this handy contrivance has fallen into disuse, there is all the more need not to keep the reader waiting. There was no necessity to do so here. What is said as a parenthesis might just as well have been said as an independent sentence following the main one.

It is not only the reader who may forget where he was when the parenthesis started. Sometimes even the writer does.

> . . . Owing to a shortage of a spare pair of wires to the underground cable (a pair of wires leading from the point near your house back to the local exchange, and thus a pair of wires essential to the provision of a telephone service for you) is lacking. . . .

The writer thought he had entered the parenthesis with the words " Owing to the fact that a spare pair of wires to the underground cable " and he continued conformably when he emerged.

PARTICULAR

This is a word that is often employed unnecessarily with the mistaken idea of emphasising a demonstrative pronoun (*this*, *that*, etc.) which needs no emphasising. Each of the following sentences is better without the word *particular* :

> In the special circumstances of this particular case the Department is willing. . . .
>
> The Department is now making enquiries in order to clarify this particular point.
>
> No arrangements have yet been made regarding moneys due to this particular country.
>
> We would point out that availabilities of this particular material are extremely limited.

See also AVAILABILITY.

> On the same day on which you advised the Custodian of the existence of this particular debt.

How easily this meaningless use of *particular* can become a habit will be apparent from a study of political speeches of a certain kind. " So far as that particular matter is concerned " (*see also* CONCERNED) is used as a sort of punctuation mark to end every paragraph.

PER

This Latin preposition should not be permitted to get too free with the English language. Such convenient abbreviations as *m.p.h.* and *r.p.m.* are no doubt with us for good. But generally it is well to confine *per* to its own language—e.g. *per cent, per capita, per stirpes, per contra*, and not to prefer *per day* to *a day*, or *per passenger train* to *by passenger train*, or *as per my letter* to *as I said in my letter.*

Even for phrases in which *per* is linked to a Latin word, there are often English equivalents which serve at least as well, if not better. A letter can equally well be signed *AB for CD* as *CD per pro AB*. £100 *a year* is more natural than £100 *per annum*. *Per se* does not ordinarily mean anything more than *by itself* or *in itself*.

PERCENTAGE, PROPORTION, FRACTION

Do not use the expression *a percentage* or *a proportion* when what you mean is *some*, as in:

> This drug has proved of much value in a percentage of cases.
>
> The London Branch of the National Association of Fire Officers, which includes a proportion of station officers. . . .

Here *percentage* and *proportion* pretend to mean something more than *some*, but do not really do so. They do not give the reader any idea of the number or proportion of the successful cases or station officers. One per cent is just as much "a percentage" as ninety-nine per cent.

Do not forget the simple words *many*, *few*, and *some*; and do not use *percentage* or *proportion* unless you want to express not an absolute number but the relation of one number to another, and can give at least an approximate degree of exactitude; so that though you may not be able to put an actual figure on the percentage or proportion, you can at any rate say "a high percentage", "a large proportion", "a low percentage", "a small proportion".

But *fraction* is different. It has become so common to use "only a fraction" in the sense of "only a small fraction" that it would be pedantry to object that $\frac{999}{1000}$ is as much a fraction as $\frac{1}{1000}$ just as it would certainly be pedantry to point out to anyone who says "He has got a temperature" that 98 degrees is just as much "a temperature" as 104.

PERUSE

Peruse has no advantage over *read*, and has the disadvantage that it gives a stiff old-fashioned air to a document:

> I suggest therefore that you forward the correspondence I am enclosing to Mr. X so that he can peruse same and take the matter up.

"Read it" is more natural and friendly than "peruse same". *See also* SAME.

> As a perusal of the Act will reveal . . .

Here again it is more natural and friendly to say "as you will see by looking at the Act".

PHENOMENAL

The proper meaning of this word is " perceptible by the senses " and a *phenomenon* is merely an occurrence that is perceptible by the senses. But these words have long been used by some writers as if they meant *prodigious* and *prodigy*. Mr. Vincent Crummles' daughter was called " the infant phenomenon " because she was, in her parents' opinion, a juvenile prodigy. This use has never been universally accepted, though it has respectable backing. It still gives some offence, and official writing should keep clear of it.

PHRASAL VERBS

The English language likes to tack a preposition to a simple verb and thus to create a verb with a different meaning. Verbs thus formed have been called by Logan Pearsall Smith, following Bradley, " phrasal verbs ". This habit of inventing phrasal verbs has been the source of great enrichment of the language. Pearsall Smith says*:

> From them we derive thousands of vivid colloquialisms and idiomatic phrases by means of which we describe the greatest variety of human actions and relations. We can take *to* people, take them *up*, take them *down*, take them *off* or take them *in*; keep *in* with them, keep them *down* or *off* or *on* or *under*; get *at* them or *round* them or *on with* them ; do *for* them, do *with* them or *without* them, and do them *in*; make *up to* them; set them *up* or *down* or hit them *off*—indeed there is hardly any action or attitude of one human being to another which cannot be expressed by means of these phrasal verbs.

But there is today a tendency to form phrasal verbs to express a meaning no different from that of the verb without the particle—of saying *meet with* instead of *meet*, *visit with* instead of *visit*, *study up* instead of *study*, *consult with* instead of *consult*, *check up*, or *check up on* where *check* would do as well and *face up to* where *face* would be enough. To do this is to debase the language, not to enrich it.

To measure up to in the sense of to be adequate to an occasion is the latest popular favourite ; whether it will establish itself as a useful addition to the language remains to be seen.

PLEASE FIND

Please find enclosed herewith . . .

Do not use this formula, a meaningless and discredited piece of commercialese. " I enclose " is all that is needed. *See* COMMERCIALESE

---

* *Words and Idioms*. Constable & Co.

POINT OF VIEW etc.

Point of view, *viewpoint*, *standpoint*, and *angle*, useful and legitimate in their proper places, are sometimes no more than a refuge from the trouble of precise thought, and provide clumsy ways of saying something that could be said more simply and effectively. They may be used, for instance, as a circumlocution for a simple adverb, such as " from a temporary point of view " for " temporarily ". Here are a few examples:

> He may lack the most essential qualities from the viewpoint of the Teaching Hospitals. (He may lack the most essential qualities for work in a Teaching Hospital.)
>
> It is a bad let-down from the customer's point of view. (Here, as often, the phrase takes the place of a simple preposition : " a bad let-down for the customer ".)
>
> The firm's production from an output point of view. (Here the context shows that " production from an output point of view " means no more than " output ".)
>
> I can therefore see no reason why we need to see these applications, apart from an information point of view. (Except for information.)
>
> This may be a source of embarrassment to the Regional Board from the viewpoint of overall planning and administration. (This is a particularly bad one. The plain way of putting it is : " This may embarrass the Regional Board in planning and administration ". For this use of *overall*, *see* OVERALL).

See also ASPECT, which, as the complement of *point of view*, leads writers astray in the same way.

POSITION (Noun)

This word is a noted sinner among those abstract words (*see* ABSTRACT WORDS) that seduce writers into complicated obscurity. Anyone who finds himself using it should treat the discovery as a danger-signal, warning him to consider whether what he wants to say cannot be said more clearly and pithily in another way. That horrible phrase " position in regard to ", should always be rejected when it proffers itself. Not content with ousting the old-fashioned " state of ", it is committing more and more outrages against clear expression. " The question of the British position in regard to the amount of authorisation " (from a high class newspaper) is today's way of saying " the question how much Britain is to get of the amount authorised ". " The position in regard to the supply of labour and materials has deteriorated " seems to come more naturally to the pen than " labour and materials are more difficult to get ". " No one has any doubt " writes the *Manchester Guardian*, " that deceased senior officials of the civil service have *in regard to* engraved on their hearts; and their successors today show no recovery from this kind of hereditary lockjaw." But it is not fair to put all the blame on officials.

Even without the company of "in regard to" *position* does much mischief.

The B.B.C. tells us of a Government spokesman:

> Dealing with the eggs position, he said that it exceeded all expectations.

What is an "eggs position", and how can it "exceed all expectations"? The spokesman presumably meant that it looked as if eggs would be more plentiful than anyone had expected. If so, why not say so?

It is common form for an Insurance Company, when asking for a renewal premium, to say:

> No-claim bonus is shown subject to the position in this respect remaining unprejudiced until expiry.

This wraps up in verbiage the simple statement that the right to the no-claim bonus is conditional on no claim being made before the expiry of the policy.

> The House was waiting to hear what Mr. Strachey had to say about the position of meat imports from Argentina.

Why drag in "position"? What the House was waiting to hear was what Mr. Strachey had to say about meat imports from Argentina.

Similarly "the position of" only cumbers the paper in:

> It has now come to the position of the manufacturers having to supply the part required.

The next example shows how ready-made phrases like "supply position" present themselves automatically as thought-savers:

> Your letter about National accounting machines has been carefully considered, but owing to the acute supply position I am sorry that I can do nothing to help you.

What the writer meant was "but as these machines are so scarce . . ."

"You will be advised in due course regarding your position" is a starchy way of saying "you will be told in due course how you stand", and "if such is the position" a very starchy way of saying "if so".

POSITION (Verb)

The verb "to position" is referred to under the heading NEW VERBS. But there are reasons why it should have a special mention.

Its history is instructive.

In 1935 Sir Alan Herbert wrote:

> A pint of bogus verbs in " tion " would make more mischief than a gallon of honest slang. I see with dismay that the verb " to position " has been admitted to the newspapers. . . . now why, Bobby, is " to position " a bad verb? Not only because we have already such verbs as " to place " and " to space " : but because " to position " is itself congenitally feeble. It is not formed from the main verb-root but from a subordinate case (the comical accusative, *positionem*, Bobby) of a noun derived from the parent-verb. It is like a very distant cousin claiming an earldom.

Fourteen years later His Majesty's Government published an illustrated advertisement to help their campaign for stimulating industrial output. The picture is of a dismayed batsman watching silly-mid-on take an easy catch. Above the picture are the words " See how POSITIONING helps PRODUCTIVITY ". Below is written:

> Watch a crack cricket side in the field. See how they're POSITIONED to stop runs and scoop up catches. They save themselves sweat by being at the right place at the right time. . . .

Under such patronage *position* may fairly claim that its battle is as good as won. But it would still be wise for humbler folk to avoid it, even at the cost of having to use three words (*put in position*) instead of one. The simple *place* is not always an adequate substitute.

POSITION (NOT IN A POSITION TO)

It would perhaps be unreasonable to condemn so time-honoured a phrase. But it is generally better to say *cannot* or *am not able* than to use this faded metaphor. Perhaps it attracts because it seems to soften the blow of refusal; it is less abrupt than those little words. But against this must be set a certain foolishness that appears in the phrase when examined. " If you are not in a position to give me what I want, why not change your position? " is the retort that will come into your correspondent's mind.

PRACTICABLE and PRACTICAL

Practical, with its implied antithesis of *theoretical*, means useful in practice. *Practicable* means capable of being carried out in action.

> That which is practicable is often not practical. Anything that is possible of accomplishment by available means may be called practicable. Only that which can be accomplished successfully or profitably under given circumstances may be called practical.
>
> (Weseen, *Words Confused and Misused*.)

PREFER

You may say " He prefers writing to dictating " or " he prefers to write rather than to dictate ", but not " he prefers to write than to dictate ".

PREPARED TO

A foolish habit has grown up recently of saying someone is "prepared" to do something when what is meant is that he is doing or even has done it. When you say "the Minister is prepared to consider your application if you will submit it in the prescribed form", that makes sense. But when you say (as I have seen over and over again) something like this : "The Minister is prepared to approve your application, and I enclose the necessary licence", that makes no sense. The preparatory stage is clearly over. Here is an example of the absurdities into which a writer can be led by this silly trick :

> I have to acknowledge your letter of the 16th June and in reply I am prepared to inform you that I am in communication with the solicitors concerned in this matter.

PREPOSITIONS

(i) Circumlocutory prepositions.

Certain phrases are overworked as general-purpose prepositions. Among them are :

As regards
As to
In connexion with
In regard to
In relation to
In respect of
In the case of
Relative to
With reference to
With regard to

They are useful in their proper places, but they are generally found outside their proper places, serving merely as clumsy devices to save a writer the labour of selecting the right preposition. I reproduce here a collection that I made for *Plain Words* with one or two additions. The right preposition is added in brackets :

> A firm time-table *in relation to* the works to be undertaken should be drawn up (for).
>
> It has been necessary to cause many dwellings to be disinfested of vermin, particularly *in respect of* the common bed-bug (of).
>
> The general attitude of modern industry *in relation to* the activities of the Government (towards).
>
> More progress has been made *in the case of* the Southern Railway and the Great Western Railway than *in the case of* the other two Companies (by).
>
> A lease was entered into *in respect of* six floors of a building (of).

The Authority are fully conscious of their responsibilities *in regard to* the preservation of amenities (for).

It will be necessary to decide the priority which should be given to nursery provision *in relation to* other forms of education provision (over).

The rates vary *in relation to* the age of the child (with).

Coupons without restrictions *as to* how you should spend (on).

There may be difficulties *with regard to* the provision of suitable staff (in).

Similar considerations apply *with regard to* application for a certificate (to).

The best possible estimate will be made at the conference *as to* the total number of houses which can be completed in each district during the year (of).

For further comments on *in regard to*, *see* POSITION (Noun).

(ii) Prepositions tacked on to verbs. *See* PHRASAL VERBS.

(iii) Ending sentences with prepositions.

Do not hesitate to end a sentence with a preposition if your ear tells you that that is where the preposition goes best. There used to be a rather half-hearted grammarian's rule against doing this, but no good writer ever heeded it, except Dryden, who seems to have invented it. The translators of the Authorised Version did not know it (" but I have a baptism to be baptised with "). The very rule itself, if phrased " do not use a preposition to end a sentence with ", has a smoother flow and a more idiomatic ring than " do not use a preposition with which to end a sentence ". Sometimes, when the final word is really a verbal particle, and the verb's meaning depends on it, the two cannot be separated. "A disturbance which half-a-dozen policemen sufficed to put down " cannot be written " a disturbance down which half-a-dozen policemen sufficed to put ". The ear is a pretty safe guide. Nearly a hundred years ago Dean Alford protested against this so-called rule. " I know ", he said, " that I am at variance with the rules taught at very respectable institutions for enabling young ladies to talk unlike their elders. But that I cannot help ".

(iv) Cannibalism by prepositions.

Cannibalism is the name given by Fowler to a vice that prepositions are specially prone to, though it may infect any part of speech. One of a pair of words swallows the other:

> Any articles for which export licences are held or for which licences have been applied.

The writer meant " or for which export licences have been applied for ", but the first *for* has swallowed the second.

PREVENT

You may choose any one of three constructions with *prevent*: *prevent him from coming*, *prevent him coming*, and *prevent his coming*.

PRIOR TO

Do not use *prior to* as a preposition instead of *before*. *Before* is simpler, better known, and more natural, and therefore preferable. It is moreover at least questionable whether *prior to* has established itself as a preposition. By all means use the phrase a *prior engagement*, where *prior* is doing its proper job as an adjective. But do not say that you made an engagement *prior to* receiving the second invitation.

> Mr. X has requested that you should submit to him, immediately prior to placing orders, lists of components . . .
>
> Sir Adrian Boult is resting prior to the forthcoming tour of the B.B.C. Symphony Orchestra.

In sentences such as these *prior to* cannot have any advantage over the straightforward *before*.

PROHIBIT

The idiom of *prohibit* is *from doing*, unlike that of *forbid*, which is *to do*.

PRONE *see* LIKELY

PRONOUNS

"The use of pronouns", said Cobbett, "is to prevent the repetition of nouns, and to make speaking and writing more rapid and less encumbered with words". In more than one respect they are difficult parts of speech to handle.

(i) It is an easy slip to use a pronoun without a true antecedent.

> He offered to resign but it was refused.

Here *it* has not a true antecedent, as it would have had if the sentence had begun "he offered his resignation". This is a purely grammatical point, but unless care is taken over it a verbal absurdity may result. Cobbett gives this example from Addison:

> There are indeed but very few who know how to be idle and innocent, or have a relish of any pleasures that are not criminal; every diversion they take is at the expense of some one virtue or other, and their very first step out of business is into vice or folly.

As Cobbett points out, the only possible antecedent to *they* and *their* is the "very few who know how to be idle and innocent", and that is exactly the opposite of what Addison means.

(ii) Be sure that there is no real ambiguity about the antecedent. This is more than a grammatical point ; it affects the intelligibility of what you write. Special care is needed when the pronouns are *he* and *him*, and more than one male person has been mentioned. Latin is sensible enough to have two pronouns for *he* and *him*, one of which is used only when referring to the subject of the sentence; but English affords no such aids.

Stevenson lamented this and said:

> When I invent a language there shall be a direct and an indirect pronoun differently declined—then writing would be some fun.
>
> | DIRECT | INDIRECT |
> | --- | --- |
> | He | Tu |
> | Him | Tum |
> | His | Tus |
>
> Example : He seized tum by tus throat ; but tu at the same time caught him by his hair. A fellow could write hurricanes with an inflection like that. Yet there would be difficulties too.*

Handicapped as we are by the lack of this useful artifice, we must be careful to leave no doubt about the antecedents of our pronouns, and must not make our readers guess, even though it may not be difficult to guess right. As Jespersen points out, a sentence like " John told Robert's son that he must help him " is theoretically capable of six different meanings. It is true that Jespersen would not have us trouble overmuch when there can be no real doubt about the antecedent, and he points out that there is little danger of misunderstanding the theoretically ambiguous sentence:

> If the baby does not thrive on raw milk, boil it.

Nevertheless, he adds, it is well to be very careful about one's pronouns.

Here are one or two examples, to show how difficult it is to avoid ambiguity:

> Mr. S. told Mr. H. he was prepared to transfer part of his allocation to his purposes provided that he received £10,000.

The *his* before *purposes* refers, it would seem, to Mr. H. and the other three pronouns to Mr. S.

> Mr. H. F. saw a man throw something from his pockets to the hens on his farm, and then twist the neck of one of them when they ran to him.

Here the change of antecedent from " the man " to Mr. H. F. and back again to " the man " is puzzling at first.

---

* Letter to E. L. Burlinghame, March 1892.

There are several possible ways of removing ambiguities such as these. Let us take by way of illustration the sentence, " Sir Henry Ponsonby informed Mr. Gladstone that the Queen had been much upset by what he had told her " and let us assume that the ambiguous *he* refers to Mr. Gladstone. We can make the antecedent plain by

1. Not using a pronoun at all, and writing " by what Mr. Gladstone had told her ".
2. Parenthetic explanation—" by what he (Mr. Gladstone) had told her ".
3. The *former-latter* device—" by what the latter had told her ".
4. By rewriting the sentence—" The Queen was much upset by what Mr. Gladstone told her, and Sir Henry Ponsonby so informed him ".
5. The device that Henry Sidgwick called " the polite alias " and Fowler " elegant variation ", and writing (say) " by what the Prime Minister had told her ", or the " G.O.M." or " the veteran statesman ".

It may safely be said that the fifth device should seldom if ever be adopted*, and the third only when the antecedent is very close. *See* FORMER and LATTER.

(iii) Do not be shy of pronouns.

So far we have been concerned in this section with the dangers that beset the user of pronouns. But for the official no less a danger is that of not using them when he ought. Legal language, which must aim above all things at removing every possible ambiguity, is more sparing of pronouns than ordinary prose, because of an ever-present fear that the antecedent may be uncertain. For instance, opening at random an Act of Parliament, I read:

> The Secretary of State may by any such regulations allow the required notice of any occurrence to which the regulations relate, instead of being sent forthwith, to be sent within the time limited by the regulations.

Anyone not writing legal language would have avoided repeating *regulations* twice; he would have put *they* in the first place and *them* in the second.

---

* This journalistic trick is out of favour now. But it used to be an accepted feature of fine writing. There is a remarkable example in the extract from *The Times* of 6th December, 1848, printed in the issue of the 6th December, 1948. The reference is to a forthcoming demonstration of M. Molk's newly-invented " electric searchlight ":

> "At this period of the evening the moon will be in its zenith, but M. Molk does not apprehend any sensible diminution of the lustre of his light from the presence of that beautiful luminary ".

Officials have so much to read and explain that is written in legal English that they become infected with pronoun-avoidance. The result is that what they write is often, in Cobbett's phrase, " more encumbered with words " than it need be.

> Arrangements are being made to continue the production of these houses for a further period, and increased numbers of these houses will, therefore, be available.

There is no reason why the second *these houses* should not have been *them*. (This is an example of encasing *therefore* in unnecessary and tiresome commas. *See* COMMA.) *See also* SUCH.

(iv) It is usually better not to allow a pronoun to precede its principal. If the pronoun comes first the reader may not know what it refers to until he arrives at the principal.

> I regret that it is not practicable, in view of its size, to provide a list of the agents.

Here, it is true, the reader is only momentarily left guessing what *its* refers to. But he would have been spared even that if the sentence had been written:

> I regret that it is not practicable to provide a list of the agents; there are too many of them.

PROPORTION *see* PERCENTAGE

PROPOSITION

Proposition should not be used as a synonym for *plan* or *project*; in England that is hardly better than slang. The ordinary meaning of the word is something put forward for discussion or as the basis of argument. Use a simple adjective—*feasible* or *practicable* rather than the phrase " a practical proposition ".

PROTAGONIST

This word is not the opposite of *antagonist* (one who contends with another); the pair must not be used as synonyms of *supporter* and *opponent*, the *pros* and the *antis*. *Protagonist* has nothing to do with the Latin word *pro*: its beginning is derived from a Greek word meaning first, and it means literally the principal actor in a play; hence it is used for the most prominent personage in any affair. It is not necessarily associated with the advocacy of anything, although it often happens to be so in fact. When we say that Mr. Willett was protagonist in the movement for summer time, we are not saying that he was *pro* summer time; we are saying that he played a leading part in the movement. *Protagonist* should never be used in the sense merely of *advocate* or *champion*.

PROVIDED THAT

This form of introduction of a stipulation is better than *provided* without the *that* and much better than *providing*. The phrase should be reserved for a true stipulation, as in:

He said he would go to the meeting provided that I went with him,

and not used loosely for *if* as in:

I expect he will come tomorrow, provided that he comes at all.

Sometimes this misuse of *provided that* creates difficulties for a reader:

Such emoluments can only count as qualifying for pension provided that they cannot be converted into cash.

The use of *provided that* obscures the meaning of a sentence that would have been clear with *if*.

PROX. *see* INST.

PURPORT (Noun)

This word is apt to be overworked. Possible alternatives are *upshot*, *gist*, *tenor*, *substance*, *pith*.

PURPORT (Verb)

The ordinary meaning of this verb is " to profess or claim by its tenor ", e.g. " this letter purports to be written by you ". The use of the verb in the passive is an objectionable and unnecessary innovation. " Statements which were purported to have been official confirmed the rumours " should be " statements which purported to be official confirmed the rumours ".

QUALIFICATION OF ABSOLUTES

Certain adjectives and adverbs cannot properly be qualified by such words as *more*, *less*, *very*, *rather*. *Unique* is the outstanding example. When we say a thing is *unique* we mean that there is nothing else of its kind in existence; *rather unique* is meaningless. But we can of course say *almost unique*.

It is easy to slip into pedantry here, and to condemn the qualification of words which are perhaps strictly absolutes but are no longer so treated—*true*, for instance, and *empty* and *full*. We ought not to shrink from saying " very true ", or " the hall was even emptier today than yesterday " or " this cupboard is fuller than that ".

QUESTION

For *Question as to*, *see* As To.

Question is overworked by indolent writers. Possible alternatives are *subject*, *topic*, *matter*, *problem*, *case*.

RE

This word, an abbreviation of *in re*, is the ablative case of the Latin word *res*. It means *in the matter of*. It is used by lawyers for the title of lawsuits, such as " in re John Doe deceased ". It has passed into commercialese (*see* COMMERCIALESE) as an equivalent of the English preposition *about*. It has no business there, or in officialese. It is not needed either in a heading (" re your application for a permit "), which can stand without its support, or in the body of a letter, where an honest *about* will serve your purpose better.

REACTION

Reaction has had a meteoric career, almost rivalling that of *overall* and *target*. It now seems to come naturally to an official writer, answering an enquiry where certain equipment can be bought, to end his letter:

> Would you therefore communicate with the XY Co. Ltd., and let me have your reaction.

Reaction may be properly used as a technical term of chemistry (the response of a substance to a reagent), of biology (the response of an organ of the body to an external stimulus), or of mechanics (" to every action there is an equal and opposite reaction "). One would think that was as much work as a word could reasonably be asked to do. Its present vogue is grievous. A word that connotes essentially an automatic rather than an intellectual response is being used habitually to replace such words as *opinion*, *views*, or *impression*. Never say " What is your reaction to this proposal ? " instead of " what do you think of this proposal ? " unless you wish to imply that the person you are questioning must answer instantly without reflection. *Reaction's* extension of its meaning was harmless at first, and even useful. One cannot quarrel with:

> I suggest that Mr. X communicates with some of the firms named with a view to testing market reactions to his products.

But the further encroachments of the word should be discouraged because they blur exactitude of meaning.

The preposition after *reaction* must be *to*, never *on*. It is permissible to say " His reaction to your letter was unfavourable ".

But it is not permissible to say " Your letter had an unfavourable reaction on him ". To say that is to imply a belief that one of the meanings of *reaction* is *effect*.

REALISTIC

This word is becoming dangerously popular, perhaps because it has a question-begging flavour. *See* BEG THE QUESTION. What is realistic is what the writer thinks sensible. A leading article in a certain journal recently said of a certain minister:

> He made great play, as he has done before, with the word " realistic " which he is in danger of associating with anything he thinks.

Realistic is ousting words like *sensible*, *practical*, *feasible*, *workmanlike*.

RECOURSE *see* RESORT

RECRUDESCENCE

This popular word should be confined to bad things such as diseases and crimes. It is an inappropriate word to use of anything pleasant or beneficent.

REDUNDANT

This is an imposing word and, no doubt for that reason, is used in senses that it will not bear. The idea of *too much* is inseparable from it; " superabundant, superfluous, excessive ", is what the dictionary says. To treat it as meaning merely *inappropriate* is wrong.

> The Authority are now reluctant to proceed with the provision of services for a 10,000 population in case their work becomes redundant due to the subsequent need for catering for a larger population.

It is nonsense to say that provision for a population of a certain size might become superabundant if it were subsequently necessary to cater for a larger population. For this use of *due to*, *see* DUE TO.

REGARD

Unlike *consider*, *count*, and *deem*, *regard* requires an *as* in such a sentence as " I regard it as an honour ".

RELATIVELY and COMPARATIVELY (and UNDULY)

Many writers, especially the official, have a trick of instinctively using one of these adverbs to qualify all adjectives of measure or quantity such as *long*, *short*, *many*, *few*, *heavy*, *light*. It is a curious habit, only to be explained by a shrinking from definite statement; and it is therefore a bad one. These words should be used only when a comparison is made with something else; they are words of exact meaning, and it is wrong to use them merely for the purpose of watering down the precision of a statement. It would not be easy to defend the adverb in:

> Today hosts of men and women earn their living by doing monotonous repetitive work which demands relatively little skill. . . .

But it is rightly used in:

> Over six hundred fresh cases of influenza have been reported but comparatively few are of a severe type.

Unduly is another adverb that seems to prompt writers to the same sort of meaningless use. In the sentence " there is no need to be unduly meticulous " *unduly* is doing no work ; the writer meant " there is no need to be meticulous ". But *unduly* contributes to the meaning in the sentence " The speech was not unduly long for so important an occasion ".

RENDITION

The original meaning, now archaic, was *surrender*, and, like *surrender* and *give up*, it could be used of either a garrison or a fugitive. The word is now less common in England than in America, where it is freely used in the sense of translation, or version, and of musical or dramatic performance. For these we in Britain still prefer *rendering*, though, with our usual disposition to imitate things American, we are giving *rendition* a run. There is no authority in either country for using the word as an all-purposes noun for the act of rendering. It is, I am told, used in this way in the Services and in some civil departments, where one may find expressions as startling even as " the rendition of this return is long overdue " as a way of saying " this return ought to have been sent in long ago ".

REPETITION

Pronouns were invented to avoid the necessity of repeating nouns. The section on PRONOUNS deals with this subject, and also with the device known as " the polite alias " or " elegant variation ".

Unnecessary repetition of a word is irritating to a reader and distracts his attention. If it can be avoided in a natural way it should be. For instance, in the sentence " The Minister has considered this application, and considers that there should be a market in Canada ", the repetition of " consider " gives the sentence a clumsy and careless air. The second one might just as well have been " thinks ". It would have been easy also to avoid the ugly repetition of *essential* in the sentence " it is essential that the Minister should have before him outline programmes of essential works ". But where the same thing or act is repeatedly mentioned, it is better to repeat a word than to avoid it in a laboured and obvious way.

Irritating repetition of a sound (assonance) is always mere carelessness.

> Reverting to the subject of the letter the latter wrote . . . (This is indefensible because it could so easily be avoided by calling " the latter " by name.)

REQUIRE

Official English shows an undue preference for *require* over its synonyms, perhaps from a mistaken feeling that *want* is too colloquial.

> Please state if you require this amount paid in full to meet your immediate requirements. (Please say whether you would like this amount paid in full to meet your immediate requirements.)
>
> I trust this will give you the information you require. (I trust this will give you the information you want.)

Require should not be used as an intransitive verb in the sense of *need* as it is in:

> You do not require to do any stamping unless you wish, (you need not) and
>
> Special arrangements require to be worked out in the light of local circumstances (special arrangements will have).

RESORT, RESOURCE, RECOURSE

There is much pardonable confusion about these words. The most common mistake is to write " have resource to " instead of " have recourse to " or " have resort to ". The correct usage can be illustrated thus:

> They had recourse (or had resort, or resorted) to their reserves; it was their last resource (or resort); they had no other resources.

RESPECTIVE and RESPECTIVELY

These words are often used wrongly and very often unnecessarily. " Of ten sentences in which they occur ", says Fowler, " nine would be improved by their removal ". Here is a recent example:

> There are many other provisions in the Act which are referred to in the respective chapters dealing with the main fields of activity of the Central Authority and the Area Boards.

They have only one useful function. That is to serve as distributors in such a sentence as:

> Please fill in both the buff and the green forms, and return them to the Ministry and the Committee respectively.

Without the *respectively* it would not be clear which authority preferred which colour. But even here the word could be dispensed with and the style of the sentence improved by writing:

> Please fill in both forms and return the buff one to the Ministry and the green one to the Committee.

There is also a harmless but unnecessary distributive use in such a sentence as:

> Local Education Authorities should survey the needs of their respective areas. . . .

It hardly seems necessary to guard against the risk that Local Authorities might think that they were being told to survey one another's areas. Anyway it is neater to write " Each Local Authority should survey the needs of its area ".

SABOTAGE

Sabotage is defined as " deliberate and organised destruction of plant, machinery, etc., by dissatisfied workmen, hence, generally, any malicious or wanton destruction ". It has come much into favour of late, especially to signify the wrecking of some project or agreement in an underhand way by one of the parties to it. Perhaps that is because there has been so much of that sort of thing going on in international affairs during the last twenty years.

The right of sabotage to be a verb is disputed. " Let us by all means sabotage the verb ", says Sir Alan Herbert, " for the robust verb *to wreck* will always do the same work better ". When *wreck*, *destroy*, or *damage* will serve as well, one of these words ought of course to be preferred. But will they always serve? They have not the same implication of disloyalty as *sabotage* has. The use of *sabotage* as a verb is recognised by the dictionaries and will take some sabotaging.

SAME

Four hundred years ago, when the Thirty-nine Articles were drawn up, it was good English idiom to use *the same* as a pronoun where we should now say *he* or *she*, *him* or *her*, *they* or *them*, or *it*.

> The riches and goods of Christians are not common, as touching the right title and possession of the same, as certain Anabaptists do falsely boast.

This is no defence for the present pronominal use of *the same* and *same*, which survives robustly in commercialese. *See* COMMERCIALESE. It is to be found to some extent in official writing also, especially in letters on business subjects. This use of *same* is now by general consent reprehensible. It should be stamped out as soon as possible, and the genuine pronouns should be restored to their proper functions.

Example	*Correction*
As you have omitted to insert your full Christian names, I shall be glad if you will advise me of same.	As you have omitted to insert your full Christian names, I shall be glad if you will let me know what they are.
With reference to the above matter, and my representative's interview of the 12th October, relative to same. . .	With reference to this matter and my representative's interview of the 12th October, about it. . .
I enclose the necessary form for agreement and shall be glad if you will kindly complete and return same at your early convenience.	(For *same* substitute *it*.)

I am informed that it may be decided by X Section that this extra will not be required. I await therefore their decision before taking further action in an attempt to provide.

I like to think that the writer stopped abruptly after *provide*, leaving it objectless, in order to check himself on the brink of writing *same*. But he might harmlessly have written *it*.

SEMI-COLON

Do not be afraid of the semi-colon; it can be most useful. It marks a longer pause, a more definite break in the sense, than the comma; at the same time it says " Here is a clause or sentence too closely related to what has gone before to be cut-off by a full-stop ". The semi-colon is a stronger version of the comma. A frequent mistake is to use a comma where two clauses without a conjunction call for a stronger stop. *See* COMMA.

The Company is doing some work on this, it may need supplementing.

If it is your own pension please say what type it is, if it is your mother's then it need not be included in your income.

Each of these sentences needs a semi-colon in place of the comma.

The semi-colon is also useful for avoiding the rather dreary trailing participles with which writers often end their sentences:

The postgraduate teaching hospitals are essentially national in their outlook, their geographical situation being merely incidental.

An attempt to devise permanent machinery for consultation was unsuccessful, the initial lukewarm response having soon disappeared.

There is nothing faulty in the grammar or syntax of these sentences, and the meaning of each is unambiguous. But they have a tired look. They can be wonderfully freshened by using the semi-colon, and rewriting them:

> The postgraduate teaching hospitals are essentially national in their outlook; their geographical situation is merely incidental.
>
> An attempt to devise permanent machinery for consultation was unsuccessful; the initial lukewarm response soon disappeared.

SENTENCES

A sentence is not easy to define. Many learned grammarians have tried, and their definitions have been torn in pieces by other learned grammarians. But what most of us understand by a sentence is what the O.E.D. calls the "popular definition": "such a portion of composition or utterance as extends from one full-stop to another". That definition is good enough for our present purposes, and the question we have to consider is what general guidance can be given to a writer about what he should put between one full-stop and the next.

The two main things to be remembered about sentences by those who want to make their meaning plain is that they should be short and should have unity of thought. Here is a series of 84 words between one full-stop and another, which violates all the canons of a good sentence. In fact it might be said to explode the definition, for it would be flattering to call it a "sentence". "This is not a sentence", said a friend who was good enough to look through this book in proof. "This is gibberish".

> Forms are only sent to applicants whose requirements exceed x, and in future, as from tomorrow, forms will only be sent to firms whose requirements exceed 5x, and as you have not indicated what your requirements are, I am not sending you forms at the moment because it is just possible that your requirements may be well within these quantities quoted, in which case you may apply direct to the usual suppliers, of which there are several, with a view to obtaining your requirements.

If we prune this of its verbiage, and split it into three short sentences, a meaning will begin to emerge.

> Only firms whose requirements exceed 5x now need forms. Others can apply direct to the suppliers. You do not say what your requirements are, so I will not send you a form unless I hear that you need one.

The following is an even worse example of a meandering stream of words masquerading as a sentence:

> Further to your letter of the above date and reference in connection with an allocation of . . ., as already pointed out to you all the allocations for this period have been closed, and I therefore regret

> that it is not possible to add to the existing allocation which has been made to you and which covers in toto your requirements for this period when originally received, by virtue of the work on which you are engaged, a rather higher percentage has been given to you namely 100 per cent of the original requirements and at this stage I am afraid it is not practicable for you to increase the requirement for the reasons already given.

The fault here is excessive verbiage rather than of combining into one sentence thoughts that ought to have been given several. The thought is simple, and can be conveyed in two sentences, if not in one:

> Your original application was granted in full because of the importance of your work. I regret that the amount cannot now be increased, as allocation for this period has been closed.

Now let us look at the other side of the picture, and examine a letter written by someone who had learned the value of short sentences. If the writer had believed in getting as much as possible between his full-stops, it might have run

> I enclose herewith the usual forms relating to new claims for sickness benefit which please return after inserting in the blank square after the N.I. number on the forms the suffix to your N.I. number which is printed on your N.I. card after the six figures.

That would be grammatical and intelligible. But it would not be readily intelligible, and the writer of this letter properly determined to make himself readily intelligible. So he made five sentences of it and wrote:

> I am sending with this letter the usual forms relating to new claims for sickness benefit. When returning them will you please insert the suffix to your N.I. number. It is printed on your N.I. card after the six figures. You will see that there is a blank square after the N.I. number on the forms. That is where the suffix should go.

This may perhaps be criticised as a trifle too staccato, and it would in fact be improved if the second sentence were joined to the third, and the fourth to the fifth, by colons or semi-colons. But the short sentences do present the reader one by one with the points that he has to take in. The full-stops seem to say to him: "Have you got that? Very well; now I'll tell you the next thing". If the sentence is long he goes on reading it to the end, never quite sure whether a point is complete, and then goes back and reads it again to disentangle the points. *See also* Full-Stop.

SERVICE

As a verb, *service* is a newcomer. In the sense either of giving periodical attention to a machine, or of providing interest and amortisation for a loan, it fills a gap and seems to have established itself in spite of opposition from high authority. But it must be kept in its place, and not allowed to usurp the functions of *serve* as it does in

> A large number of depots of one sort or another will be required to service the town, and
>
> To enable a Local Authority to take advantage of this provision it is essential that sites should be available, ready serviced with roads and sewers.

SHALL and WILL

Twenty pages devoted to this subject in *The King's English* begin with the following introduction:

> It is unfortunate that the idiomatic use, while it comes by nature to southern Englishmen (who will find most of this section superfluous), is so complicated that those who are not to the manner born can hardly acquire it; and for them the section is in danger of being useless. In apology for the length of these remarks it must be said that the short and simple directions often given are worse than useless. The observant reader soon loses faith in them from their constant failure to take him right; and the unobservant is the victim of false security.

The author's view in short amounts to this: that if anyone has been brought up among those who use the right idiom, he has no need of instruction; if he has not, he is incapable of being instructed, because any guidance that is short and clear will mislead him and any that is full and accurate will be incomprehensible to him.

Every English text-book will be found to begin by stating the rule that to express the "plain" future *shall* is used in the first person and *will* in the second and third:

I shall go
You will go
He will go

and that if it is a matter not of plain future but of volition, permission or obligation it is the other way round:

I will go (I am determined to go)
You shall go (You must go, or you are permitted to go)
He shall go (He must go, or he is permitted to go)

But the idiom of the Celts is different. They have never recognised "I shall go". For them "I will go" is the plain future. American practice follows the Celtic, and in this matter, as in so many others, the English have taken to imitating the American. If we go by practice rather than by precept, we can no longer say dogmatically that "I will go" for the plain future is wrong. The Commissioner of Police for the Metropolis is reported to have said:

> When police manpower shortage is solved we will have an answer

> to the desperate men now willing to maim and murder. Give policemen houses, and we shall have more recruits.

He uses first *will* and then *shall* for the plain future in the first person, showing a fine impartiality. That is typical of present-day practice in England. We can no longer say smugly with Dean Alford:

> I never knew an Englishman who misplaced *shall* and *will*; I hardly ever have known an Irishman or Scotchman who did not misplace them sometimes.

The Irish and the Scots are having their revenge for our bland assumption that English usage must be "right" and theirs "wrong".

Nevertheless, the rule for the official must be to be orthodox on doubtful points of doctrine, and text-book orthodoxy still prescribes *shall* with the first person to express the plain future. So we must judge the second thoughts of the Commissioner of Police to have been best.

SHORT SUPPLY

"In short supply" is the fashionable phrase nowadays. When so many things are scarce, it is no doubt excusable to seek variety in the ways of saying so. But the invention of this inelegant expression has had the opposite effect, for it has driven all rivals off the field. It would be a relief to go back to "scarce" occasionally. Let us hope that the introduction of Sir Short Supply as one of the Itma characters did something to debunk this cliché.

SINGULAR and PLURAL VERBS

The rule that a singular subject requires a singular verb, and a plural subject a plural verb, is an easy one to remember and generally to observe. But it has its incidental difficulties.

(i) Collective words.

About collective nouns, or nouns of multitude (Department, Parliament, Government, committee, and the like), *see* COLLECTIVE WORDS.

(ii) Words linked by *and*.

To the elementary rule that two singular nouns linked by *and* should be given a plural verb justifiable exceptions can be found where the linked words form a single idea. The stock example is Kipling's "The tumult and the shouting dies"; "the tumult and the shouting", it is explained, are equivalent to "the tumultuous shouting".

Perhaps these official examples might be justified in the same way:

> Duration and charge was advised at the conclusion of the call.
>
> Your desire and need for a telephone service is fully appreciated.

It might be argued that " duration and charge " was equivalent to " the appropriate charge for that duration ", and that " your desire and need " was equivalent to " the desire arising from your need ". But it is safer to observe the rule, and to leave these questionable experiments to the poets.

Other instances of singular verbs with subjects linked by *and* cannot be so easily explained away. They are frequent when the verb comes first. Shakespeare has them (" Is Bushy, Green and the Earl of Wiltshire dead ? ") and so have the translators of the Bible (" Thine is the kingdom, the power and the glory "). If we may never attribute mere carelessness to great writers, we must explain these by saying that the singular verb is more vivid, and should be understood as repeated with each noun—" Is Bushy, (is) Green, and (is) the Earl of Wiltshire dead ? " Those who like to have everything tidy may get some satisfaction from this, but the writer of official English should forget about these refinements. He should stick to the simple rule. *See also* THERE IS.

(iii) Words linked by *with*.

If the subject is singular the verb should be singular. " The Secretary of State together with the Under Secretary is coming ", not " are coming ".

(iv) Alternative subjects.

If both are singular the verb is singular, and if both are plural the verb is plural.

> Either the Secretary of State or the Under Secretary is coming.
>
> Either the Ministers or their officials are coming.

If one is singular and the other plural the verb usually takes the number of the one nearest it (" either the Minister or his officials are coming "), but if we want to be scrupulously logical we must have two verbs and write:

> Either the Minister is coming or his officials are.

(v) Attraction.

The verb must agree with the subject, and not allow itself to be attracted into the number of the complement. Modern grammarians will not pass " the wages of sin is death ". The safe rule for the ordinary writer in sentences such as this is to regard what precedes the verb as the subject and what follows it as the complement, and so to write " the wages of sin are death " and " death is the wages of sin ".

A verb some way from its subject is sometimes lured away from its proper number by a noun closer to it, as in:

> We regret that assurances given us twelve months ago that a sufficient supply of suitable local labour would be available to meet our requirements has not been fulfilled.
>
> The Minister's views in general . . . and the nature and scope of the information which he felt would assist him . . . was indicated at a meeting. . . .

Sometimes the weight of a plural pushes the verb into the wrong number, even though they are not next to one another:

> Thousands of pounds' worth of damage have been done to the apple crop.

In these sentences *has*, *was*, and *have* are blunders. So is the common attraction of the verb into the plural when the subject is *either* or *neither* in such sentences as " Neither of the questions have been answered " or " Either of the questions were embarrassing ". But in one or two exceptional instances the force of this attraction has conquered the grammarians. With the phrase *more than one* the pull of *one* is so strong that the singular is always used (e.g. " more than one question was asked "), and owing to the pull of the plural in such a sentence as " none of the questions were answered " *none* has come to be used indifferently with a singular or a plural verb.

SORT *see* KIND

SPECIAL PLEADING

This used to be a respectable term of the law. In passing into common use it has degenerated, and now means something little different from sophistry, quibbling argument.

SPECIFIC

Like *definite* (*see* DEFINITE) this is an adjective that tends to be used unnecessarily by way of emphasising some quality that needs no emphasis because it is inherent in the noun qualified. It is often used superfluously as an epithet of such words as *decision*, *directions*, *rules*, *ruling*, *regulations*.

SPLIT INFINITIVE

The well-known grammarians' rule against splitting an infinitive means that nothing must come between *to* and the verb. It is a cramping rule; it increases the difficulty of writing clearly it;

makes for ambiguity; and I know of no justification for its existence that can be put in the scale against these disadvantages. The commonest way in which it creates ambiguity is this: that if, let us say, you are forbidden to write "he failed to completely convince them" you will probably write "he failed completely to convince them". Your reader will then not be sure whether you mean "he completely failed to convince" or "he failed to completely convince", and they are obviously very different things.

Nor is this all. The split-infinitive taboo, leading as it does to the putting of adverbs in awkward places, is so potent that it produces an impulse to put them there even though there is not really any question of avoiding a split infinitive. I have myself been taken to task by a correspondent for splitting an infinitive because I wrote "I gratefully record". He was, no doubt, under the influence of the taboo to an exceptional extent. But sufferers from the same malady in a milder form can be found on every hand. We cannot doubt that the writer of the sentence "they appeared completely to have adjusted themselves to it" put the adverb in that uncomfortable position because he thought that to write "to have completely adjusted" would be to split an infinitive. The same fear, probably subconscious, may also be presumed to account for the unnatural placing of the adverb in "so tangled is the web that I cannot pretend for a moment that we have succeeded entirely in unweaving it". In this there is no possibility of splitting an infinitive because there is no infinitive. But the split infinitive bogy is having such a devastating effect that people are beginning to feel that it must be wrong to put an adverb between any auxiliary and any part of a verb, or any preposition and any part of a verb.

The infinitive can be split only by inserting a word or words between the word which, with *to*, forms the infinitive of the verb. "To fully understand" is a split infinitive. So is "to fully have understood". But "to have fully understood" is not.

In *Plain Words* I wrote of the rule against the split infinitive:

> Still, there is no doubt that the rule at present holds sway, and on my principle the official has no choice but to conform; for his readers will almost certainly attribute departures from it to ignorance of it, and so, being moved to disdain of the writer, will not be "affected precisely as he wishes".

A friend whose opinion I value has reproached me for this, making no secret of his view that I am little better than a coward. I ought, he tells me, to have the courage of my convictions. I ought to say about the split infinitive, as I said about the "inanimate whose", that it is right for the official to give a lead in freeing writers from this fetish. The furthest I ought to allow myself to go along the road of safety-first is, according to him, to say that it is judicious for an official to avoid splitting whenever he can do so without sacrificing clarity, ease, and naturalness of expression. But rather than make that sacrifice he should resolutely split.

My friend may be right.

STAGE (AT THIS STAGE)

At this stage is becoming an official cliché. Do not write it when all you mean is *now*.

STANDPOINT *see* POINT OF VIEW

STEPS

" Take steps to " is often padding, and should be used with care. It is not always to be condemned. It is a reasonable way of expressing the beginning of a gradual process, as in:

> Steps are now being taken to acquire this land.

But it is inapposite, because of its literal incongruity, in such a sentence as:

> All necessary steps should be taken to maintain the present position.

STERILISE

This word means to make unfruitful. It has come much into favour recently among officials to express the idea of a veto on the use of something for a profitable purpose, and shows signs of the usual usurping tendencies of such words; you may already find examples of *sterilised* used merely as a synonym for *wasted*. It also needs watching for another reason. To speak of sterilising coal needed for the support of buildings is to use an appropriate metaphor; the coal is being made unfruitful for the purposes for which we use coal. But to speak of sterilising land in the sense of preventing its being built on is to say exactly the opposite of what you mean: the land is being preserved in order that it may continue to be fruitful.

SUBJUNCTIVE

The subjunctive is the mood of imagination or command. Apart from the verb *to be*, it has no form separate from the indicative, except in the third person singular of the present tense, where the subjunctive form is the same as the indicative plural (*he have*, not *he has*; *he go*, not *he goes*). Generally therefore, in sentences in which the subjunctive might be appropriate, neither the writer nor the reader need know or care whether the subjunctive is being used or not.

But the verb *to be* spoils this simple picture. The whole of the present tense is different, for the subjunctive mood is *be* throughout—*I be*, *he be*, *we be*, *you be* and *they be*. The singular (but not the plural) of the past tense is also different—*I were* and *he were* instead of *I was* and *he was*. In the subjunctive mood what looks like the past tense does not denote pastness ; it denotes a greater call on the imagination. Thus :

> " If he is here " implies that it is as likely as not that he is.
> " If he be here " is an archaic way of saying " if he is here ".
> " If he were here " implies that he is not.

The subjunctive is dying ; the indicative is superseding it more and more. Its only remaining regular uses are :

(*a*) In certain stock phrases : " Be it so ", " God bless you ", " come what may ", " if need be " and others.

(*b*) In legal or quasi-legal language : " I move that Mr. Smith be appointed Secretary ".

(*c*) In conditional sentences where the hypothesis is not a fact :

> Were this true, it would be a serious matter.
> If he were here I would tell him what I think of him.

(*d*) With *as if* and *as though*, if the hypothesis is not accepted as true, thus :

> He spoke of his proposal as if it were a complete solution of the difficulty.

Other correct uses of the subjunctive may be found in contemporary writings, but it is probably true of all of them that the indicative would have been equally correct, and certainly true of many of them that the subjunctive has a formal, even pedantic, air. Jespersen says :

> In the old language the subjunctive served in clauses to express various subjective moods, uncertainty, hesitation, diffidence, etc. But these feelings are no longer felt with the same force as formerly, and as the subjunctive is hardly ever used colloquially, it may now, to a great extent, be considered a literary trick to remove the style from everyday associations.

SUBSTITUTE

To *substitute* means to put a person or thing in the place of another ; it does not mean to take the place of another. When

A is removed and *B* is put in its place, *B* is substituted for *A*, and *A* is replaced by *B*. We may write:

> The Minister has substituted Jones for Smith as a member of the committee,

but we must not write:

> Jones has substituted Smith as a member of the committee

or:

> Smith has been substituted by Jones as a member of the committee.

In the last two sentences the verb needed is *replaced.*

SUCH

Official prose is made unnecessarily ugly by a shyness of pronouns. *See* PRONOUNS. Instead of using them, writers are given to repeating the noun, often embroidered by *such.*

> If you owe debts to French concerns it is necessary for you to report such debts to the Department. . . . (them)

This " such "-disease, endemic in the civil service, is due to infection by legal English. There, this use of " such " is not a disease, but an indispensable device for securing economy of words. The draftsman, whose concern is to make his meaning certain beyond the possibility of error, first defines the sense in which he is using a word, and afterwards, when he has to use it again in the same sense, puts *such* before it, or surrounds it with *such . . . as aforesaid*, so that he need not repeat the definition. There is no reason for the official to be so punctilious.

But using *such* in the way the lawyers use it is not always out of place in ordinary writing. Sometimes it is proper and useful.

> One month's notice in writing must be given to terminate this agreement. As no such notice has been received from you . . .

Here it is important for the writer to make it clear that in the second sentence he is referring to the same sort of notice as in the first, and the *such* device is the neatest way of doing it.

As such is sometimes used in a way that seems to have no meaning:

> The statistics, as such, add little to our information.

If they do not do so as statistics, in what capacity do they? The writer probably meant " by themselves ".

SUCH and SO

> It will take some time to unravel such a complicated case.

There are those who say that this is unidiomatic, and that we ought to say " so complicated a case ". But if we choose to regard them as pedants we shall have Fowler on our side, and so cannot be far wrong.

SUCH AS and SUCH THAT

The difference between the idiomatic uses of these expressions may be illustrated thus:

> The complications of this case are *such as will take some time to unravel.*
>
> The complications of this case are *such that they will take some time to unravel* or *such that it will take some time to unravel them.*

Such as may legitimately be treated as a pronoun-preposition: we may write " I would not do it for such as him " and need not insist pedantically on " I would not do it for such as he (is) ".

SUCH TIME AS (UNTIL and DURING) *see* UNTIL

SUFFICIENT

Do not use the word *sufficient* unless you have some better reason for doing so than that you think it more dignified than *enough.* Do not, for instance, say *sufficiently frequently* when you might say *often enough.*

TARGET

Of all the words that have been called on to help in the restoration of our balance of trade, *target* has been the most in demand. No doubt it was chosen as a vivid means of denoting something for which our existing vocabulary provided only dull words like *objective* or *aim.* There is no uplift in inciting an industry to " attain its objective ". *Goal* was a possible alternative, but not so picturesque. And if *target* was to have all the stimulating force it was capable of, it would not do to treat it as a live metaphor, and exhort people to do nothing more exciting or enterprising than merely to hit it. So we were offered a great variety of things that we might meritoriously do to our targets. We might reach them, achieve them, attain them or obtain them ; we were to feel greatly encouraged if we came in sight of the target to which we were trying to do whatever we were trying to do, and correspondingly depressed if we found ourselves either a long way behind it or (what apparently amounts to the same thing) a long way short of it. On the other hand it would be splendid to be a long way beyond it. Above all we must not mistake a target for a ceiling, but must realise that it was a platform from which to climb.

At first this caused some perplexity, and even evoked some ribaldry among old-fashioned people who thought of a target as something to be hit, as nearly as possible in the middle, by a missile of some sort, and as of not much use for any other purpose. But we are past all that now. Target, as part of our post-war economic jargon, is a dead metaphor; we may use with it any verb that we might use with *objective*, and our jokes have become pedantry.

But we ought not to be tried too hard. A lecturer has recorded that, when he read in a speech by one of our ministers of a "global target" which, to the minister's regret, could not be "broken down", the picture that came into his mind was of a drunken reveller attacking a Belisha Beacon. When we are told that the target has been doubled it still needs a little mental adjustment to realise that it will present a task twice as difficult, not, as one might have thought, twice as easy. And we cannot help being momentarily puzzled on finding that a warning by the Prime Minister that a dock strike was "imperilling the possibility of obtaining our six months' export target" is given a headline "ATTLEE SAYS EXPORT TARGET HIT". *See also* BREAKDOWN, GLOBAL and METAPHOR.

TENSES (SEQUENCE OF TENSES)

A common piece of carelessness is to write "I shall be glad if you would do so-and-so" or "I should be glad if you will do so-and-so". These are clumsy and illiterate. They should be "I shall be glad if you will . . ."; "I should be glad if you would". For more on the sequence of tenses, *see* INDIRECT STATEMENT.

THAN

Than tempts writers to use it as a preposition, like *but* (*see* BUT), in such a sentence as "he is older than me". Examples can be found in good writers. But the compilers of the "Oxford English Dictionary" will not have it. We must say "he is older than I" (i.e. than I am). We may say "I know more about her than him" if what we mean is that my knowledge of her is greater than my knowledge of him, but if we mean that my knowledge of her is greater than his knowledge of her, we must say "I know more about her than he (does)".

But one exception is recognised—whom. We must say "than whom", and not "than who", even though the only way of making grammatical sense of it is to regard *than* as a preposition. But that is rather a stilted way of writing, and can best be left to poetry:

> Beelzebub . . . than whom, Satan except, none higher sat.

Be careful not to slip into using *than* with words that take a different construction. *Other* and *else* are the only words besides comparatives that take *than*. *Than* is sometimes mistakenly used with such words as *preferable* and *different*, and sometimes in place of *as*:

> Nearly twice as many people die under twenty in France than in Great Britain, chiefly of tuberculosis.

THAT

That is an awkward word because it may be one of three parts of speech—a conjunction, a relative pronoun, and a demonstrative pronoun. "I think that the paper that he wants is that one" illustrates the three in the order given. More than one modern writer has tried the experiment of spelling the word differently (*that* and *thatt*) according to its function; but not all readers are likely to find this expedient helpful, and any official who used it would be likely to get into trouble.

It is a sound rule that *that* should be dispensed with whenever this can be done without loss of clarity or dignity. For instance the sentence just given might be written with only one *that* instead of three: "I think the paper he wants is that one". Some verbs seem to need a conjunctive *that* after them more than others do. *Think* is one that can generally do without. The more formal words like *state* and *assert* cannot. As to the omission of the relative *that*, *see* WHICH AND THAT.

The conjunctive *that* often leads writers into error, especially in long sentences. This is not so much a matter of rule as of being careful. Here are some examples:

> It was agreed that, since suitable accommodation was now available in a convenient position, and that a move to larger offices was therefore feasible, Treasury sanction should be sought for acquiring them.

Here a superfluous *that* has slipped into the middle of the sentence. The first *that* was capable of doing all the work.

> All removing residential subscribers are required to sign the special condition, that if called upon to share your line that you will do so.

That is another case of careless duplication.

> As stated by the Minister of Fuel and Power on the 8th April, a standard ration will be available for use from 1st June, 1948, in every private car and motor-cycle currently licensed and that an amount equivalent to the standard ration will be deducted . . .

The draftsman of this forgot how he had begun his sentence. He continued it as though he had begun " The Minister of Fuel and Power stated . . ." instead of "As stated by the Minister of Fuel and Power ". The consequence was that he put in a *that* which defies both sense and grammar.

> Their intention was probably to remove from the mind of the native that he was in any way bound to work, and that the government would protect him from bad employers.

This example shows the need of care in sentences in which *that* has to be repeated. If you do not remember what words introduced the first *that*, you may easily find yourself, as here, saying the opposite of what you mean. What this writer meant to say was that the intention was to remove the first idea from the native's mind and to put the second into it, not, as he has accidentally said, to remove both.

It is good idiom, though not always elegant, to use the relative *that* as equivalent to *which* with a preposition, as in:

> During the two years that these works are under construction (during which).
>
> Owing to the pace that the car was going . . . (at which).

THE MORE etc.

The with a single comparative always indicates that a reason is to be given, and must not be followed, like a plain comparative, by *than*.

> He is the more willing to sanction Smith's appointment because he knows him well.

If we want to construct such a sentence with a *than*, we must omit the *the*, e.g.:

> He is more willing to sanction Smith's appointment than he would be if he did not know him well.

The with a pair of comparatives always means " by so much as . . . by that much ".

> The nearer you get to the one, the further you are likely to find yourself from the other.

THERE IS and THERE ARE

It is a common slip to write *there is* or *there was* where a plural subject requires *there are* or *there were*.

There was available one large room and three small ones.

Was should be *were*.

It is true that Ophelia said " there is pansies ". But she was not herself at the time.

THERETO, THEREWITH etc. *see* HERETO, HEREWITH etc.

THEY for HE OR SHE

It is common in speech, and not unknown in serious writing, to use *they* or *them* as the equivalent of a singular pronoun of a common sex, as in : " Each insisted on their own point of view, and hence the marriage came to an end ". This is stigmatised by grammarians as a usage grammatically indefensible. It ought, they would say, to have been " He insisted on his own point of view and she on hers ". Jespersen says about this:

> In the third person it would have been very convenient to have a common-sex pronoun, but as a matter of fact English has none and must therefore use one of the three makeshift expedients shown in the following sentences :
>
> The reader's heart—if he or she have any. (Fielding).
>
> He that hath ears to hear let him hear. (A. V.).
>
> Nobody prevents you, do they ? (Thackeray).

The official writer will be wise for the present to use the first or second, and not to be tempted by the greater convenience of the third, though necessity may eventually force it into the category of accepted idiom. The Ministry of Labour and National Service have invented another device, but it is an ugly one, suitable only for forms :

> Each worker must acknowledge receipt by entering the serial number of the supplementary coupon sheet issued to him/her in column 4 and signing his/her name in column 5.

Whatever justification there may be for using *themselves* as a singular common-sex pronoun, there can be no excuse for it when only one sex is concerned.

> The female manipulative jobs are of a type to which by no means everyone can adapt themselves with ease.

There is no reason why *herself* should not have been written instead of *themselves*.

TRANSMIT

Prefer *send* if that is what you mean. *Transmit* has its own useful work to do which no other word can do as well. Hereditary traits may be transmitted from parent to child, light may be transmitted through glass, and power may be transmitted by means of shafts and belts. *Transmit* should not be put to the menial service of sending enclosures with letters.

TRANSPIRE

It is a common error to use transpire as if it meant *happen* or *occur*. It does not. It means *to become known*.

ULT. *see* INST.

UN

There are occasions when a writer's meaning may be conveyed more exactly by (say) *not unkindly*, *not unnaturally* or *not unjustifiably*, than by *kindly*, *naturally* or *justifiably*. But the " not un- " habit is liable to take charge, with disastrous effects, making the victim forget all straightforward adjectives and adverbs. George Orwell recommended that we should all inoculate ourselves against the disease by memorising this sentence : "A not unblack dog was chasing a not unsmall rabbit across a not ungreen field ". *See also* DE and DIS and NON for the practice of creating new words by what are called " privative prefixes ".

UNATTACHED GERUND *see* ING ENDINGS

UNATTACHED PARTICIPLE *see* ING ENDINGS

UNDULY *see* RELATIVELY.

UNEQUAL

The idiom is unequal *to*, not *for*, a task.

UNILATERAL, MULTILATERAL, BILATERAL

These words are not for everyday use. They have long been part of the jargon of the diplomatist and the physiologist. And they have recently been admitted into that of the economist, where they are doing much hard work. But for ordinary purposes it is best to stick to *one-sided*, *many-sided* and *two-sided*.

> Dr. J. M. described the condition of a man in a Southwark court case as " bilateral periorbital haematoma and left subjunctival haemorrhage ". Asked what this meant he replied : " For we ordinary mortals, two lovely black eyes ". (*Evening Standard*, 2nd March, 1949.)

It is a pity that the doctor marred the moral by saying " for we ordinary mortals ".

UNINTERESTED *see* DISINTERESTED.

UNIQUE *see* QUALIFICATION OF ABSOLUTES

UNTIL

(i) *Unless and until.* In this combination as in the combination *if and when* (*see* IF AND WHEN), one of the conjunctions is almost always superfluous. So make up your mind which expresses your meaning better, and rely on it alone.

(ii) *Until such time.*

> You will be able to enjoy these facilities until such time that he terminates his agreement.

In this sentence, and probably in every imaginable sentence, *until* is enough without the *such time.* If you insist nevertheless on writing *until such time,* the phrase should be *such time as,* not *such time that.* Similarly *while* is preferable to *during such time as.*

UTILISE and UTILISATION

These words are hardly ever needed, for the simple word *use* will almost always serve. The official (not a government official) who wrote " This document is forwarded herewith for the favour of your utilisation " should have written " please use this form ". That says what needed to be said in four syllables instead of twenty-one.

Nor is there any reason for preferring the longer word in :

> The sum so released may, upon receipt of same, be utilized to reimburse you for expenses.

For the phrase " upon receipt of same ", *see* SAME.

Certainly *use* and *utilise* should not be employed merely by way of " elegant variation "* as they apparently are in :

> It is expected that Boards will be able to utilise the accommodation now being used by the existing governing bodies.

VERBAL and ORAL

Some authorities hold that " *verbal* means ' couched in words ', spoken or written as the case may be, and is not synonymous with *oral,* ' delivered by word of mouth ' ". It would no doubt be convenient if this were so, for it would make for greater precision of language. But it is not : there is ample authority for the common use of *verbal* to distinguish the spoken word from the written.

VERBAL PARTICLES *see* PHRASAL VERBS

---

* See footnote to p.114.

VERBS, OMISSION OF

Where a verb is used with more than one auxiliary (e.g. " he must and shall go ") make sure that the main verb is repeated unless, as in this example, its form is the same. It is easy to slip into such a sentence as:

> The steps which those responsible can and are at present taking to remedy this state of affairs.

Can taking makes no sense. The proper construction is shown in:

> The board must take, and are in fact taking, all possible steps to maintain production.

VERY

(i) Be sparing of *very*. If the word is used too freely it ceases to have any meaning ; it must be used with discrimination to be effective. *See* ADVERBS.

(ii) One of the most popular objects of the chase among amateur hunters of so-called grammatical mistakes used to be *very* with a past participle—" very pleased " for instance. It is true that *very* cannot be used grammatically with a past participle—that one cannot for instance say " The effect was very enhanced " ; we must say *much* or *greatly*. But when the participle is no longer serving as a verb, and has become in effect an adjective, it is legitimate to use *very* with it as with any other adjective. There can be no objection to " very pleased ", which means no more than " very glad ", or to " very annoyed ", which means no more than " very angry ". But it will not do to say " very inconvenienced " or " very removed ", and in between are doubtful cases where it will be as well to be on the safe side and refrain from *very*.

VIEWPOINT *see* POINT OF VIEW

WASTE and WASTAGE

There is a difference between these two words that ought to be preserved ; wastage should not be used as a more dignified alternative to waste. The ordinary meaning of waste is " useless expenditure or consumption, squandering (of money, time, etc.) ". The ordinary meaning of wastage is " loss by use, decay, evaporation, leakage, or the like ". You may for instance properly say that the daily wastage of a reservoir is so many gallons. But you must not say that a contributory factor is the wastage of water by householders if what you mean is that householders waste it.

WHAT

What, in the sense of *that which*, or *those which*, is an antecedent and relative combined. Because it may be either singular or plural in number, and either subjective or objective in case, it needs careful handling.

Its difficulties of number can be solved by asking the question " what does it stand for ? "

> What is needed is more rooms.

Here *what* means *the thing that*, and the singular verb is right.

On the other hand, in the sentence " He no doubt acted with what are in his opinion excellent reasons " *are* is right because *what* is equivalent to *reasons that.*

Because *what* may be subjective or objective writers may find themselves making the same word do duty in both cases, a practice condemned by grammarians. For instance:

> This was what came into his head and he said without thinking.

What is here being made to do duty both as the subject of *came* and as the object of *said*. We must write either :

> This is what (subjective) came into his head and what (objective) he said without thinking, or, preferably,
>
> This is what came into his head, and he said it without thinking.

WHEN

It is sometimes confusing to use *when* as the equivalent of *and then.*

> Will you please forward the necessary evidence . . . and an explanation of the reason for delay when the matter will receive immediate attention. (If you will forward . . . the matter will . . .)
>
> The certificate should be forwarded to the Local Office at the earliest possible moment when the claim will receive immediate attention. (Please forward the certificate to the Local Office as soon as possible. The claim will then receive. . . .)
>
> I would suggest that you complete the attached form of application when your claim will be fully investigated. (If you will complete . . . your claim will . . .)
>
> Let me have full particulars when I will be able to advise you. (Please let me have full particulars. I shall then be able to advise you.)
>
> Alternatively the Minister may make the order himself when it has the same effect as if it has been made by the Local Authority. (. . . the Minister may make the order himself, and it has the same effect, etc. . . .)

WHICH

The New Yorker of the 4th December, 1948, quoted a question asked of *The Philadelphia Bulletin*:

> My class would appreciate a discussion of the wrong use of *which* in sentences like " He wrecked the car which was due to his carelessness ",

and the answer given by that newspaper:

> The fault lies in using *which* to refer to the statement " *He wrecked the car* ". When *which* follows a noun it refers to that noun as its antecedent. Therefore in the foregoing sentence it is stated that the car was due to his carelessness, which is nonsense.

What is ? Carelessness ? is the *New Yorker's* query.

Which shows how dangerous it is to dogmatise about the use of *which* with an antecedent consisting not of a single word but of a phrase.*

The fact is that this is a common and convenient usage, but needs to be handled discreetly to avoid ambiguity or awkwardness.

> The required statement is in course of preparation and will be forwarded as soon as official records are complete, which will be in about a week's time.

Here it is unnecessary ; the sentence can be improved by omitting the words " which will be ", and so getting rid of the relative altogether.

> The long delay may make it inevitable for the authorities to consider placing the order elsewhere which can only be in the United States which is a step we should be anxious to avoid.

Here the writer has succeeded in using *which* in this way twice in a single sentence, and shown how awkward its effect can be. He might have put a full-stop after *elsewhere* and continued " That can only be in the United States and is a step we should be anxious to avoid ".

WHICH and THAT

On the whole it makes for smoothness of writing not to use the relative *which* where *that* would do as well, and not to use either if a sentence makes sense and runs pleasantly without. But that is a very broad general statement, subject to many exceptions.

That cannot be used in a " commenting "† clause ; the relative must be *which*. With a " defining "† clause either *which* or *that* is permissible, but *that* is to be preferred. When in a " defining "

---

* *Punch* has also provided an illustration of the same danger (" from a novel ") :

> Mrs. Brandon took the heavy piece of silk from the table, unfolded it, and displayed an altar cloth of her own exquisite embroidery . . . upon which everyone began to blow their nose . . .

† These terms are explained on page 30.

clause the relative is in the objective case, it can often be left out altogether. Thus we have the three variants :

> This case ought to go to the Home Office, *which* deals with police establishments. (Commenting relative clause.)
>
> The Department *that* deals with police establishments is the Home Office. (Defining relative clause.)
>
> This is the case you said we ought to send to the Home Office. (Defining relative clause in which the relative pronoun, if it were expressed, would be in the objective case.)

WHILE

It is safest to use this conjunction only in its temporal sense (" Your letter came while I was away on leave "). That does not mean that it is wrong to use it also as a conjunction without any temporal sense, equivalent to *although* (" while I do not agree with you, I accept your ruling "). But it should not be used in these two different senses in the same sentence, as in :

> While appreciating your difficulties while your mother is seriously ill . . .

Moreover, once we leave the shelter of the temporal sense, we are on the road to treating *while* as a synonym for *and*:

> Nothing will be available for some time for the desired improvement, while the general supply of linoleum to new offices may have to cease when existing stocks have run out.

There is no point in saying *while* when you mean *and.* If you are too free with *while* you are sure sooner or later to land yourself in the absurdity of seeming to say that two events occurred simultaneously which could not possibly have done so.

> The great Ohio flood . . . in 1937 which attained a height of over 65 feet developed in a week, while the almost identical amount of rain of the previous year produced a highwater mark of no more than 39 feet 3 inches.
>
> H.M.S. *Consort* is due this morning in Shanghai while H.M.S. *London* was steaming last night upstream to help the *Amethyst.*

WHO and WHOM

Who is the subjective case and *whom* the objective. The proper use of the two words should present no difficulty. But we are so unaccustomed to different case-formations in English that when we are confronted with them we are liable to lose our heads. In the matter of *who* and *whom* good writers have for centuries been perverse in refusing to do what the grammarians tell them. They will insist on writing sentences like " Who should I see there ? " (Addison), " Ferdinand whom they suppose is drowned " (Shakespeare), " Whom say men that I am ? " (Translators of the Bible). Now any schoolboy can see that, by the rules, *who* in the first quotation, being the object of *see*, ought to be *whom*, and that *whom* in the second and third quotations, being in the one the subject of *is*, and in the other the complement of *am*, ought to be *who*. What then is the ordinary man to believe? There are some who would have us do away with *whom* altogether, as nothing but a mischief-maker. That might be a useful way out. But then, as was asked in the correspondence columns of the *Spectator* by one who signed himself " A. Woodowl " (31st December, 1948):

> Regarding the suggested disuse of *whom*, may I ask by who a lead can be given? To who, to wit, of the " cultured " authorities can we appeal to boo *whom* and to boom *who*?

Whom will take some killing, too. Shakespeare and the Translators of the Bible have their distinguished followers today, such as Mr. Winston Churchill (" The slaves of the lamp . . . render faithful service to whomsoever holds the talisman "*), Mr. E. M. Forster ("A creature whom we pretend is here already "†) and Lord David Cecil (" West, whom he knew would never be seduced away from him "‡).§

But it has not yet become pedantic—at any rate in writing—to use *who* and *whom* in what grammarians would call the correct way, and the ordinary writer should so use them, ignoring these vagaries of the great. He should be specially careful about such sentences as:

> The manager should select those officers who (not whom) he desires should sign on his behalf.
>
> The manager should select those officers whom (not who) he authorises to sign on his behalf.
>
> There has been some argument about who (not whom) should be authorised to sign on the manager's behalf.

See also THAN.

WHOSE

There is a grammarians' rule that *whose* must not be used of inanimate objects: we may say " authors whose books are famous ", but we must not say " books whose authors are famous "; we must fall back on an ugly roundabout way of putting it, and say " books the authors of which are famous ".

* *Lord Randolph Churchill.*

† *Spectator*, 22nd November, 1935.

‡ *Two Quiet Lives.*

§ Sometimes, though more rarely, the opposite mistake is made:

> A Chancellor who, grudging as was the acknowledgment he received for it, everyone knew to have saved his party.

So say the grammarians. But the rule is so cramping and so pointless that the more broad-minded among them are in revolt. Fowler says, for instance, " to ask a man to write flexible English but forbid him *whose* ' as a relative pronoun of the inanimate ' is like sending a soldier on active service and insisting that his tunic and collar shall be too tight. . . . Let us in the name of common-sense prohibit the prohibition of *whose inanimate* ".

There are signs that Fowler's advice is now being followed:

> The hospital whose characteristics and associations link it with a particular religious denomination.
>
> That revolution the full force of whose effects we are beginning to feel.
>
> There has been built up a single centrally organised blood-transfusion service whose object is . . .

WORTH

Worth (compare LIKE) has a prepositional force, and needs an object. This object may be either *while* (i.e. the spending of time) or something else. It is therefore correct to say : " this job is worth while " ; it is also correct to say " this job is worth doing ". But one object is enough, and so it is wrong to say : " this job is worth while doing ".

Worth-while as an adjective (" a worth-while job ") has not yet reached more than colloquial status.

WOULD

" In reply to your letter of . . . I would inform you . . ." is a common way of beginning official letters that do not need to be in the full-dress official style of " I am directed . . ." In this phrase *would* is not a mere auxiliary expressing the conditional mood ; it retains the now archaic meaning of " I should like to ". On another page I have deprecated the use of this expression on the ground that, since it is archaic, it cannot help being stiff. *See* LETTERS.

Because *would* has this meaning, grammarians condemn such phrases as " I would like to ", " I would be glad if ", " I would be obliged if ", and so on. *Should*, they say ought always to be used : to say *would* is tantamount to saying " I should like to like to ", " I should like to be glad if ", " I should like to be obliged if ", and so on. Here, as in the use of *will* and *shall* with the first person (*see* SHALL and WILL), practice, under the lead of the Celts and Americans, is fast getting the better of the grammarians. But the grammarians should be respected by the British official, and the intrusion of *would* upon *should* ought not to be encouraged.

" It would appear " and " I should think " are less dogmatic, and therefore more polite, ways of saying " it appears " and " I think ".

WRITE

Write has the peculiarity that it must not have an indirect object unless it has a direct one too. We must not say: " I wrote you about it a week ago "; it must be " I wrote *to* you about it a week ago ". But we may say: " I wrote you a letter about it a week ago ".

E41203 Wt.4528 K.520+80